Democratization in Africa: African Views, African Voices

Summary of Three Workshops

Sahr John Kpundeh, editor

Panel on Issues in Democratization
Commission on Behavioral and Social Sciences and Education
National Research Council

National Academy Press
Washington, D.C. 1992

NOTICE: The project that is the subject of this report was approved by the Governing Board of the National Research Council, whose members are drawn from the councils of the National Academy of Sciences, the National Academy of Engineering, and the Institute of Medicine. The members of the committee responsible for the report were chosen for their special competences and with regard for appropriate balance.

This report has been reviewed by a group other than the authors according to procedures approved by a Report Review Committee consisting of members of the National Academy of Sciences, the National Academy of Engineering, and the Institute of Medicine.

The National Academy of Sciences is a private, nonprofit, self-perpetuating society of distinguished scholars engaged in scientific and engineering research, dedicated to the further-ance of science and technology and to their use for the general welfare. Upon the authority of the charter granted to it by the Congress in 1863, the Academy has a mandate that requires it to advise the federal government on scientific and technical matters. Dr. Frank Press is president of the National Academy of Sciences.

The National Academy of Engineering was established in 1964, under the charter of the National Academy of Sciences, as a parallel organization of outstanding engineers. It is autonomous in its administration and in the selection of its members, sharing with the National Academy of Sciences the responsibility for advising the federal government. The National Academy of Engineering also sponsors engineering programs aimed at meeting national needs, encourages education and research, and recognizes the superior achievements of engineers. Dr. Robert M. White is president of the National Academy of Engineering.

The Institute of Medicine was established in 1970 by the National Academy of Sciences to secure the service of eminent members of appropriate professions in the examination of policy matters pertaining to the health of the public. The Institute acts under the responsibility given to the National Academy of Sciences by its congressional charter to be an adviser to the federal government and, upon its own initiative, to identify issues of medical care, research, and education. Dr. Kenneth I. Shine is president of the Institute of Medicine.

The National Research Council was established by the National Academy of Sciences in 1916 to associate the broad community of science and technology with the Academy's pur-poses of furthering knowledge and of advising the federal government. Functioning in accor-dance with the general policies determined by the Academy, the Council has become the principal operating agency of both the National Academy of Sciences and the National Acad-emy of Engineering in providing services to the government, the public, and the scientific and engineering communities. The Council is administered jointly by both Academies and the Institute of Medicine. Dr. Frank Press and Dr. Robert M. White are chairman and vice chairman, respectively, of the National Research Council.

The work that provided the basis for this volume was supported by the U.S. Agency for International Development.

Library onf Congress Catalog Card No. 92-62337

International Standard Book Number 0-309-04797-8

B046

Available from: Panel on Issues in Democratization, Commission on Behavioral and Social Sciences and Education, National Research Council, 2101 Constitution Ave., N.W., Washing-ton, D.C. 20418

Also available for sale from: National Academy Press, 2101 Constitution Ave., N.W., Wash-ington, D.C. 20418

Printed in the United States of America

PANEL ON ISSUES IN DEMOCRATIZATION

PHILIP CONVERSE *(Chair)*, Center for Advanced Study in the Behavioral Sciences, Stanford, California

ROBERT DAHL, Department of Political Science (emeritus), Yale University

ALBERT FISHLOW, Department of Economics, University of California, Berkeley

JAMES LOWELL GIBBS, Jr. Department of Anthropology, Stanford University

ALEX INKELES, Hoover Institution and Department of Sociology (emeritus), Stanford University

ADAM PRZEWORSKI, Department of Political Science, University of Chicago

PHILIPPE C. SCHMITTER, Department of Political Science, Stanford University

ALFRED STEPAN, Department of Political Science, Columbia University

IVAN SZELENYI, Department of Sociology, University of California, Los Angeles

SIDNEY VERBA, Department of Political Science, Harvard University

DAVID M. TRUBEK, Department of International Studies and Programs and School of Law, University of Wisconsin

JO HUSBANDS, *Project Director* (through March 1992)
SABRI SAYARI, *Project Director*
SAHR JOHN KPUNDEH, *Senior Research Associate*
MARY E. THOMAS, *Senior Program Associate*

Preface

The Africa Bureau of the U.S. Agency for International Development (A.I.D.) requested assistance from the National Academy of Sciences/National Research Council in obtaining the views of leading African scholars, intellectuals, and political activists on the broad question of democratization in Africa and how A.I.D. might most appropriately support that process. In responding to this request, the National Research Council organized three workshops in Africa, drawing participants from most countries on the continent. This was an unusual and challenging undertaking for the National Research Council, and it could not have succeeded without the support and cooperation of the U.S. Department of State, particularly the embassy and A.I.D. officials in the countries that hosted our workshops, Benin, Ethiopia, and Namibia.

We are indebted to the Africans who accepted our invitations to the three workshops. The difficulties of travel in Africa required not only a very significant time commitment from the participants, but also, often, airline flights of several days' duration and multiple stops. More important, a large number of participants came at considerable personal risk—the very act of attending a meeting on democracy being an act of political defiance in their home countries. For these sacrifices of time and comfort and acts of bravery, we are very grateful.

There are also those individuals and organizations whose contributions were so important to our ability to organize the meetings and conduct them successfully that we wish to express special thanks. The University of

Benin provided support in co-organizing the first workshop; the rector of the university, Dr. Jean Pierre Ezin, was especially helpful. Tessy Bakary offered a summary of the Benin workshop on national television, in French, with less than an hour's notice. Dr. J. Isawa Eliagwu, professor of political science at the University of Jos in Nigeria, and Dr. Dele Olowu, professor of political science at Obafemi Awolowo University in Nigeria, attended two of the workshops and provided invaluable cross-fertilization from the Benin meeting to the meetings in Ethiopia and Namibia, respectively.

The Inter-Africa Group in Addis Ababa was instrumental to assuring the success of the meeting in that city, and Abdul Mohammed was tireless and unfailingly innovative in overcoming major and minor crises. Asmelash Bayene of the Economic Commission for Africa paved the way for our use of the Africa Center in Addis Ababa and in many other ways contributed to the success of the workshop. Dr. Hugh Africa of the University of Namibia provided invaluable advice and introductions that overcame many potential problems in Namibia, and Dr. Peter Katjavivi, vice chancellor designate of the University of Namibia, was not only a participant in the Windhoek meeting, but cleared many obstacles to its success that would have otherwise proved very difficult to manage.

Dr. Christopher Clapham of the Politics and International Relations Department of Lancaster University in the United Kingdom gave generously of his time to attend both the Addis Ababa and Windhoek meetings, and in both he played key roles as rapporteur and chair of several small group sessions. His insights moved the discussions along on many occasions. Teresa Smith de Cherif dazzled participants in both Addis Ababa and Windhoek with her comprehensive and accurate summaries of the daily sessions; she also contributed significantly to the writing of the workshop report, particularly the section on institutions needed to sustain democracy. Finally, Mary Thomas of the National Research Council staff proved to be a magician in accomplishing impossible logistics and solving the myriad—and totally unpredictable—problems that arose in transit and at the meeting sites. Without her unflagging efforts, the project could never have succeeded.

The Africa workshops were developed by Jo Husbands, the project director for the panel. Sahr Kpundeh was the staff officer in charge of the execution of the project and of writing the summary report. The project was conducted under the supervision of Susanne A. Stoiber, director of the Division of Social and Economic Studies of the Commission on Behavioral and Social Sciences and Education.

Philip Converse, *Chair*
Panel on Issues in Democratization

Contents

Background and Purpose
of the Workshops

The collapse of communism in the Soviet Union and the ending of the cold war has created opportunities for democratic transitions, not only in Europe and the former Soviet Union, but also in Africa. The East-West competition in Africa that provided support or at least protection for authoritarian governments came to an end. The model of a one-party state controlling all sectors of the economy was demonstrably bankrupt—not only in the Soviet Union, but throughout the African continent—as the economies of country after country disintegrated. A sea change in political and economic systems was gaining support in Africa. General Obasanjo, a former Nigerian head of state, as chairman of a conference of the African Leadership Forum in April 1990, commented:

> The changes taking place in Eastern Europe have far-reaching political implications for the Third World in general and for Africa in particular. The winds that swept away dictatorships and autocratic one-party systems and State structures, inefficient economic systems and unresponsive social institutions in Eastern Europe, and fueled a democratic rejuvenation and the observance of human rights, are not unfamiliar to Africa. The winds of change in Eastern Europe are providing considerable opportunities for the African people and oppressed peoples the world over to intensify their just struggle for democracy.

Accordingly, the U.S. Agency for International Development (A.I.D.) has expanded its efforts to encourage and support transitions from authoritarian rule to democracy and from state-administered to market-driven economies.

1

In this undertaking, A.I.D. recognizes that political and economic transitions will be influenced by each country's particular history, culture, and traditions; and that the paths taken in Latin America, Southern Europe or Eastern Europe may not necessarily be those that will be followed in Africa.

In order to better understand the dynamics of contemporary democratic movements in Africa and African opinions about how democracy can be most effectively encouraged, A.I.D. asked the National Academy of Sciences, through the National Research Council's Panel on Issues in Democratization, to organize three workshops in Africa. Held in January through March 1992, the workshops involved participants from over 40 African countries. Those attending included scholars, government officials, officers from nongovernmental organizations, journalists, lawyers, and political activists. They had in common a record of involvement on behalf of improved social conditions, political freedoms, and human rights. The first workshop was held in Cotonou, Benin; the second in Addis Ababa, Ethiopia; and the third in Windhoek, Namibia.

The format of the workshops was to use current research on various aspects of democratization as a springboard for discussions about the prospects for democratization in Africa and the role that donors, such as A.I.D., might play in supporting that process. The theme of the three workshops was "Democratization in Africa: African Views, African Voices." The agenda was broadly similar in each meeting, with some variation to take into consideration the particular concerns of the individual regions. Although the emphasis of the discussions varied somewhat by region, there was a remarkable degree of consensus in all three gatherings as to the issues that will be most important in determining whether the move towards democracy in Africa will be sustained in the coming decades. This report is an attempt to synthesize the key issues in the three workshops and to capture the highlights of what proved to be an intense and often exhilarating series of discussions.

Throughout this volume every effort has been made to let African views, perspectives, and words speak for themselves, as they did in the workshops. However, because the political climate in certain countries could imperil the personal safety of citizens who openly express controversial views and their remarks could be used against them, the consensus of the group was not to identify each speaker in the published proceedings. In compiling this volume, great care has been taken to present faithfully the words spoken without revealing the speakers' identities. In this way, we hope to convey the excitement of the discussions without jeopardizing the safety of those who participated.

1

The Movement Toward Democracy in Africa

The workshops were convened against the background of what many observers have called the "second wave of liberation in Africa." Authoritarian regimes are being challenged by individuals and movements in search of more democratic forms of governance. Africans in many countries are showing remarkable persistence in forcing their leaders to comply with popular demands for political pluralism to replace the common one-party regimes. Calls for open and democratic governance, characterized by popular participation, competitive elections, and free flow of information can be heard in many African countries.

This new disposition toward democratization in Africa is a consequence of pressures both internal and external to African societies. To be sure, the continent's declining economic fortunes have made people more skeptical and critical of their governments, with new African thinking prompting individuals to move beyond old taboos. Demands from within African countries are pressing leaders to deliver on the promises of economic growth and prosperity they made in order to encourage the acceptance of structural adjustment policies supported by international financial institutions. The new insistence by external aid donors and creditors on good governance also has provided a window of opportunity for African democrats to push for transparency and accountability in their countries. Likewise, the world-wide democratic revolution and its corresponding summons to protect and promote individual human rights have contributed to generating protests from outside the African continent against regimes accused of encouraging corrupt practices and committing human rights abuses.

In the past, Western aid donors accepted the justification that Africans endorsed authoritarian rule, but now they increasingly express their preference for countries with representative government and a good record on human rights. This new attitude was reflected in recent remarks made by former Ambassador Thomas R. Pickering, U.S. permanent representative to the United Nations: "It is not our role to decide who governs any country, but we will use our influence to encourage governments to get their people to make that decision for themselves." In the future, it is likely that Western donors will be selective with their assistance, focusing on countries undertaking both political and economic reforms.

This thinking is also shared by some former African heads of state, prominent Africans, and African organizations that have become increasingly resentful of corruption, repression, human rights abuses, and gross economic mismanagement under one-party rule. For example, the Secretary General of the Organization of African Unity (OAU), Salim Ahmed Salim, and the former Tanzanian president, Julius Nyerere, were among the many prominent African and other international statesmen involved in the Stockholm Initiative on Global Security and Governance held in April 1991. Its Memorandum on Common Responsibility in the 1990s states: "Certain democratic requisites are crucial to sustain development. . . . The following are necessary parts of the concept: respect for human rights; constitutional government and the rule of law; transparency in the wielding of power, and accountability of those who exercise power." The memorandum points out that, although democracy has to evolve from within a society, there is nevertheless "a duty for the international community to support the respect for human rights and the development of democracy. Human solidarity demands it . . ."

Furthermore, the OAU has shifted its emphasis from decolonization and is now giving priority to economic recovery and good governance. At the twenty-sixth OAU summit in 1990, OAU Secretary General Salim Ahmed Salim spoke in favor of democratization: "Africa could not ignore the global consensus on the value of democracy; but democracy must be home-grown." When President Ibrahim Babangida of Nigeria delivered his speech as incoming OAU chairman in June 1991, democratization figured prominently. He stressed that, in the process of development, Africans faced the simultaneous tasks "of solving acute problems of economic restructuring and of creating free and democratic institutions for social expression." He told fellow leaders that they "must recognize that the time has now come to re-examine the concept and practice of power and leadership on our continent. . . . Democracy is not only an attractive option but a rational one. . . .

Today, the clamour for democratization and party pluralism is on the ascendancy in Africa."

In this "second wave of liberation" across the continent, Africa is rediscovering itself through intensifying struggles for democracy. Yet support for democracy in Africa is not new, having been a common ingredient of nationalist politics at the end of the colonial era. Those few years constituted an important period of self-determination that many Africans believe should not be separated from the current quest for democracy. Only recently, however, has the demand for democracy focused once again on political pluralism, respect for human rights, official accountability, and popular participation.

A common theme in the three workshops was the reminder that democratic concepts are not alien to the African continent, despite the impression created in the postcolonial period. Democratic forms and institutions existed in precolonial African societies, and their practice may be found today in some rural areas. For example, as a form of checks and balances, some nations exercised limits on the absolute power of their leaders by electing and removing African kings. Many rulers had to consult with community leaders before implementing vital decisions. Traditionally, popular participation was encouraged by using a process of consultation that allowed African leaders to reinvigorate their rule with community input. These examples, in the view of the workshop participants, demonstrate how traditional rulers in some African societies could not enforce obedience without the consent of their advisers and ultimately of the community itself. In the postcolonial period, too, democracy did take root in several African countries, such as Botswana, The Gambia, and Mauritius, where competing political parties, an independent judiciary, and a free press have been in existence for a number of years.

Still, participants cautioned that the movement toward political pluralism in Africa is not universally endorsed. Entrenched leaders resist change, but they have often been obliged to make at least some concessions to appease donors and domestic critics. For example, Kenya's President Daniel arap Moi denounced multiparty advocates and vehemently criticized those who proclaimed political liberalization. When external assistance was all but terminated, however, he reversed his earlier position to declare on December 2, 1991, his support for multipartyism. Similarly, President Robert Mugabe of Zimbabwe was moving his country toward creating a de jure one-party state, until donor nations and outspoken individuals in Zimbabwe persuaded the government to abandon the process.

In the early postindependence phase, people justified one-party systems as national unifiers or as vanguards to unite diverse ethnic, linguistic, and religious groups; but, thirty years later, these arguments are being discarded.

Today, many African countries are moving in a democratic direction, even though the degree of commitment and speed of change vary considerably.

The problems of instituting democratic government in Africa include overcoming the resistance of entrenched governments to the pressures of local activists and aid donors, consolidating political changes, and legitimating democratic concepts in Africa. Nevertheless, over the last few years, there have been successful revolts against authoritarian leaders in Ethiopia, Somalia, Mali, and Lesotho. In addition, long, drawn-out wars for self-determination such as the Eritrean and West Saharan conflicts have terminated hostilities and are now engaged in preparation for referendum. Competitive politics also has reemerged in some states with the democratic replacement of leaders through the ballot box, as the cases of Benin, Sao Tomé and Príncipe, Cape Verde, and Zambia illustrate. For these reasons, the workshop participants expressed some degree of confidence that the changes taking place would have a better opportunity for success than the transitions from colonial rule.

IMPACT OF NEW EXTERNAL ACTORS

Although pressures for change had been building in a number of countries, it was widely agreed that the ending of the cold war served as a catalyst for action. During the cold war, some countries capitalized on superpower competition, seeking military and development assistance from either the Soviet Union and its allies or from the West in exchange for strategic considerations. The Soviet Union, like the People's Republic of China, also provided an alternative development model for African states to emulate. The end of the cold war has left the leaders of these countries exposed and scrambling to establish a new set of relationships on the continent and in the world community. One person observed: "For the African heads of state who played Western and Eastern support against each other, the collapse of the Soviet Union came as a shock. . . . African states now have to either rely on themselves or submit to external pressures for democratic reforms."

There was agreement in the three workshops that African dictators will find it harder to justify authoritarian rule and dictatorships and increasingly difficult to maintain power. In short, the impact of internal events within some African countries, coupled with external pressures from donors, had direct and indirect effects on the democratization process. Certainly, as one participant commented, the "globalization of ideas and the myriad of changes in the world have emboldened African individuals to speak up." The failure of authoritarianism has opened up the possibility of democracy's providing a new start in Africa.

COLONIAL LEGACY AND DEMOCRATIC DEVELOPMENT
IN AFRICAN SOCIETIES

The process of democratization in Africa, several participants pointed out, includes confronting the past. The colonial legacy is significant to the understanding of postindependence erosion of democratic institutions. Some participants, however, took exception to an emphasis on the precolonial past, cautioning that one should not glorify the past in order to justify present mistakes: "Turning too often to the past betrays a fundamental problem, in that we cannot deal with the present. . . . As Africans, we try to turn to the past when we wish to maintain our illusions."

Nevertheless, participants stressed that colonialism was not a democratic system and that the so-called colonial masters were not teachers of democracy because "they took self-governance away from Africans." As one participant stated, "The colonial experience was one of a minority imposing its will on a majority—a colonial apartheid, in which there were European and non-European areas in some countries, and where there was legislation for Europeans, but the Africans were relegated to customary law." Participants were also resentful that former colonial rulers are now showing little patience or understanding about African politics, largely because of Africa's declining strategic importance in world politics in recent years, forgetting that they were the ones who took away Africans' dignity and self-respect, "maintaining they were too incompetent to understand their own rights."

It was also argued by many participants that colonialism had destroyed indigenous democratic values and institutions without building stable replacements. Examples of the community palaver[1] and the Botswanan *kgotla*[2] were given. Some participants argued that colonialism had disrupted these traditional African practices. African family life, which some believed was based on equality, freedom, and unity, was overshadowed by the authoritarian and centralized nature of colonialism. However, other participants noted that colonialism did not entirely destroy indigenous practices. They argued that the survival of some African traditions and their vitality, especially the *kgotla* was one of the continuing bases for Botswanan democracy. Furthermore, they pointed out that legislative sessions and debates in francophone and anglophone Africa resemble the traditional palaver modes.

---

[1] Palaver basically refers to a dialogue or discussion in which everyone expresses an opinion, after which the minority opinion complies with that of the majority, thereby making the decision taken unanimous.

[2] *Kgotla* basically functions like a judicial organ to resolve and hear cases. Generally, it had the right to overthrow the chief; the colonial government used the *kgotla* as a way of challenging the chief. It was formerly used exclusively in dealing with adult males, but it now includes women and even younger men and minority groups.

In trying to understand the African past, it was suggested that certain continuities and discontinuities about the colonial period needed to be understood. In other words, to what extent did the pattern of colonial administration shape the politics of African nations after independence? Colonial rulers, participants pointed out, never pretended to be democratic; they were autocratic and tried to destroy indigenous structures of traditional societies. Furthermore, the colonists did not build institutions that could contribute to democratization, such as labor unions, African ecumenical movements, or other nongovernmental organizations. Some participants disagreed with this view, arguing that labor unions were legalized, even encouraged in parts of francophone and anglophone Africa after World War II, between 1946 and 1960. Ecumenical movements, such as the transterritorial parties in West Africa, they argued, also arose with varied colonial support.

The artificiality of Africa's boundaries and of the societies within them was mentioned by participants as an additional problem to deal with in their transition to democracy. In other words, the question was raised whether the creation of democracy is liable to lead to the dissolution of existing African states, or whether it will strengthen and preserve them. This is certainly an existing issue in northeast Africa, and opinion was divided among participants on this issue.

One participant observed: "In their mission to transform an artificially carved colony into a nation-state, the colonists did not recognize any modernity in indigenous knowledge," primarily because they believed the task of nation building had to come from above. Also, the autocratic nature of colonialism conflicted with African power sharing. Traditionally, one particular group could not hold power for too long, the army was recruited from outside the ruling family, and members of the local population often were incorporated as advisers. African royalty was tightly governed by tradition—kings followed custom or risked removal. Some African systems also respected the rights of women and human rights in general.

Despite the relevance of the past to the contemporary democratization process, the participants agreed that discussions should also focus on the shortcomings of precolonial Africa, as well as on the democratic heritage that had been lost. Participants noted the difficulty of agreeing on the applicability of precolonial democratic concepts today. Some participants argued that traditional practices were not democratic as such. Not all palavers, for example, were inclusionary. Moreover, in African consensus politics, there was no tradition of an opposition. Still other characteristics of precolonial Africa that do not lend themselves to democracy are that the individual was not at the center of society and that political succession and rotation in power were not peaceful and routine matters. There was agreement in the three workshops that the traditional roles and responsibilities of women, for example, are inconsistent with current concepts of democracy.

Today, some practices retained from the precolonial period, such as the traditional zero-sum nature of African politics and the fragile transitional period when one head of state succeeds another, were also identified as obstacles to democracy. New institutional arrangements are needed to choose rulers, to check their power, and to remove them. One participant noted that this should not be an impossible task, as many African languages had proverbs reflecting the notion of "finding the necessary power to limit power." There was also agreement that a new approach was needed to replace the current winner-take-all practice in Africa.

Although the precolonial rulers were blamed for improperly schooling Africans, it was acknowledged that certain basic rights that were present in the precolonial period are today being denied in many African countries. Participants pointed out that, during the period preceding independence, there was solidarity among Africans regarding the freedoms implicit in the call for self-determination, but authoritarian regimes had succeeded in repressing individuals and organizations that later espoused those freedoms in their opposition to single-party rule in African countries.

DEMOCRACY AND AFRICAN VALUES

In the three workshops, there was a striking amount of consensus on certain experiences and assumptions. Participants agreed that democracy is not the exclusive property of the West; it can be found in almost all cultures. Yet defining democracy proved elusive, as the forms for expressing it remain controversial in many African countries. Does democracy necessarily mean Western democracy? Is there only a single model for every country, regardless of its traditions and conditions? In answering these questions, participants agreed that "democracy is not a luxury for Africans" but a necessity if people are to lead free and secure lives. The authoritarian state in Africa, which is a postindependence revival of the colonial state, corresponds to economic stagnation and disintegration. Democracy, participants suggested, should therefore be regarded as a process to tackle problems, but should not be seen as a solution to all of Africa's problems. Still, a clear understanding is needed among Africans as to the kind of democracy being suggested by donors: "Are donors advocating Western democracy or democracy that will take into consideration African values and traditions?"

In linking democracy with African values, participants pointed out that, although there are certain essential principles of democracy, "Africa has to define democracy in its own way." They noted contradictions between Western and African understandings of some democratic concepts, such as political pluralism and the parliamentary mode of politics. Although they recognized that the African state must be divested of its monopoly on power to allow for a vibrant and functioning opposition, they cautioned against replacing dictatorships with democracy in form, but not in content. For example, not all political parties emerging in Africa today are genuine, many having been created by the state. In order to break down the deep-rooted primacy of the African chief, some advocated the Indian arrangement of parliament's being the supreme power, rather than the semipresidential French or U.S. systems of parliamentary politics with a strong executive. Participants pointed out that Western countries often advocate their own system of democracy but, if Africans develop their conception of democracy, it ought not be considered inferior to that of the West. In this round of liberation, they said that no amount of external assistance or advice would make up for the lack of African initiatives.

In all the workshops, there was wide agreement that Africans ought to draw on elements within their societies to give local relevance to democratic concepts, rather than run the risk of having democracy transplanted without adaptation, as was done with technology. Western democratic concepts and ideals have been borrowed before without success. Although the idea of the openness of Africa to external ideas is not unique, external ideas would prove more helpful if they were modified to blend with African values, ensuring proper understanding by the populace. Participants warned against accepting lessons so easily from countries that have long experience with democracy, when Africa has experienced only three decades of independence. As one participant suggested, "If we want democracy to exist in the African continent, we as Africans will have to keep on inventing democracy. . . . The constant reinvention of democracy based on African initiatives is what is needed in Africa."

Participants advocated "building democracy with local materials, and from the bottom up, because democracy will not succeed until people at the grass roots understand and participate in it." Africans seek to redefine democracy in local terms, to solve problems by drawing on their own ideas, and not to rely on borrowed Western ideas. "We ought not think that the concepts are so sacred and understandable only to a few. . . . We need to examine our population and polities as they are, and then look at what we want to achieve."

The time dimension of making progress toward democratization was also examined. Because of heterogeneity within African countries, participants warned against not repeating the mistakes of the end of the colonial period, when there was insufficient time provided to understanding Western concepts, institutions, and practices. The challenge is to instill democratic values and elements into African society, utilizing the African values that can imbue democracy with local relevance but not allowing the call to invent African democracy to be a cover for repression. Africans would probably institute their own timetable for moving toward democracy, which would be a long and painful process. Western countries were asked to be patient, understanding the problems impeding democracy, and contributing, where they could, to democratic transitions.

POLITICAL LIBERALIZATION AND DEMOCRATIZATION

As the decade of the 1990s is being called the age of political liberalization and democratization, participants felt the need to address the differences between the two. Political liberalization cannot be equated with democratization. Instituting political liberalization in a country, participants pointed out, would not necessarily achieve political pluralism, because such liberalization could be used by authoritarian regimes to create sham democracies. This type of liberalization entails the partial opening of an authoritarian system, short of choosing governmental leaders through competitive elections. The dismantling of authoritarian regimes was recognized as a major step toward democracy, but some participants were not convinced that a climate of liberalization would produce political pluralism. Democratization, in contrast to political liberalization, involves bringing about the end of undemocratic regimes and the beginning of consolidation of a democratic system. The overall process of democratization is usually long, painful, and complex.

The discussions about political liberalization and democratization focused on leaders, such as Daniel arap Moi of Kenya, who see liberalization as a way of defusing the opposition without fully democratizing the regime. These leaders do not wish to introduce fully participatory, competitive elections that may result in their loss of power, and some are even unsure of how far they really want to go toward political pluralism in their countries. It was noted that in South Africa, for example, "liberalization has opened up the political arena, but democratization has been postponed. . . . Political and social forces were being released without elections to determine who offered substantial leadership. In the absence of elections, this sorting out is occurring in an atmosphere of violence, coercion, and intimidation."

In conclusion, it could be maintained that democracy—in concept, if not in reality—has gained new popularity and wider acceptance as a political alternative in Africa. Multiparty democracy has become the rallying cry for much-pursued political reforms, but, in a larger sense, the agitation in Africa in the last three years stemmed from a modest question of accountability: How to hold leaders responsible for their conduct in office and how to make governments more responsive to the wishes of the people. African people need answers to these questions after decades of corrupt, indifferent, or harmful governance under single-party dictatorships. It seems that democracy is the only option that can provide the framework through which these questions can be answered.

2

Transitions to Democracy in Africa

As authoritarian regimes in Africa increasingly are being challenged across the continent, participants were hopeful that competitive multiparty systems might emerge in Africa. Nevertheless, they pointed out that emerging democratic governments would have to confront a legacy of poverty, illiteracy, militarization, and underdevelopment produced by incompetent or corrupt governments. Some wondered if the new demands being placed on African nations by international donor institutions as well as heightened individual expectations for better lives could be met by the nascent democracies.

Participants indicated that, although contemporary authoritarian regimes in Africa have taken a number of forms, they fall within the general models of one-party systems, personal dictatorships, and military regimes. The postcolonial trend toward one-party systems in Africa was justified on a number of grounds, including the alleged tradition of a single unchallenged chief, the idea of a democratic majority expressed through a single party, and the need for unity in the face of ethnic, linguistic, and cultural differences. Competitive politics was rejected as an imported luxury neither needed nor affordable in developing countries. In Malawi, for example, the idea of an opposition was rejected on quasi-theological grounds: "There is no opposition in Heaven. God himself does not want opposition—that is why he chased Satan away. Why should Kamuzu [President Banda] have opposition?"[3]

In a number of African countries, participants pointed out that the national liberation movement had evolved into a party that either legally or effectively monopolized power, often under the banner of preserving independence from foreign interference. Access to power was through the party organization and its rule was enforced through ideological persuasion or coercion. The governing party became the instrument of elite groups that held onto power at all costs and were unwilling to tolerate dissent or serious competition.

In the three workshops, much consideration was given to how, over time, the postcolonial government of newly independent African states had evolved into domination by a single party in a one-party system, which in turn often became a personal dictatorship. It was pointed out that power in the state had depended on access or proximity to, dependence on, or support from the dictator. In some cases, military dictatorships were created by coups d'état, which overthrew democratic or civilian governments. The military leaders exercised power on an institutional basis, governing collegially as a junta or by circulating top government positions among military generals. There was clear agreement that, whatever the form, one-party states and other forms of dictatorships suppressed both competition and participation, undermining the potential for a healthy civil society and the necessary institutions for democracy.

Participants recognized that in many African countries the institutions of civil society and democratic government are weaker today than they were in the immediate postindependence period, making the transition to democracy a daunting challenge. Some argued that, in order for democracy to succeed, power must shift from authoritarian and military rulers to leaders who would be representative of and sensitive to the diverse ethnic groups in African societies. These new leaders, they said, must direct a move to the protection of civil rights, establishment of agreed-upon modes of governance, and greater political accountability in order to sustain the move to democracy.

There was agreement among participants that the period of postcolonial suppression had produced a broad-based popular understanding of the need to share power and to have the ability to hold governments accountable for their actions. Nevertheless, some thought that this new thinking, although necessary, was not a sufficient basis on which to start building democracy. As Larry Diamond has argued, "It is unrealistic to think that countries in

---

[3] Decalo, S. (1992) The process, prospects and constraints of democratization in Africa. *African Affairs* 91:10.

Africa can suddenly reverse course and institutionalize stable democratic government simply by changing leaders, constitutions and/or public mentalities. If progress is made toward developing democratic government, it is likely to be gradual, messy, fitful and slow, with many imperfections along the way."[4]

MODES OF TRANSITION IN AFRICA

Although the nature and circumstances vary from one country to another, two basic patterns in the modes of transition to democracy were identified. Transitions from above occur when functioning rulers respond to an impending or actual crisis by initiating democratic reforms. Transitions from below occur when there are mounting popular pressures from the people resulting in national conferences, popular revolutions, coups d'état, or pact formations, all with the goal of moving toward a more democratic society.

Some scholars argue that transitions from above are more promising in terms of their ability to "deliver" democracy, because they tend to be more specific about their time frame, procedural steps, and overall strategy. Transitions from below are said to be plagued with a great deal of uncertainty. Other writers contend that every historical case of regime change has involved some negotiation—explicit or implicit, overt or covert—between government and opposition groups. Transitions may also begin as one type and become another, particularly if the government is unsure of how far it wants to go in opening up the country. In many cases, however, they combine elements of the two transition processes.

The participants analyzed the behavior of entrenched leaders with reference to transitions that had occurred elsewhere, finding that some African leaders still had the ability to suppress or, at least, retard democratic transitions. One observed that "much will depend on the government leaders who will be in power during the transition phase to democracy. They can set the stage for a peaceful and democratic change, or can obstruct the entire process." Another view was that "we ought to be cautious not to expect much from governments [in creating a conducive climate] in this process. Most are unlikely to give up their position of power and advantage." With regard to discussions concerning the overthrow of African dictators, some participants said that the point was not whether citizens had the right to overthrow authoritarian or dictatorial governments, but whether the dictators removed would be replaced by democratic regimes. One com-

---

[4] Diamond, L. (1989) Beyond autocracy: Prospects for democracy in Africa. *Beyond Autocracy in Africa*, p. 24. Atlanta: The Carter Center of Emory University.

mented: "We have to examine certain principles in the constitution to see what kinds of guarantees they offer as far as the limitation of power is concerned."

Participants agreed that where authoritarian governments had suppressed the evolution of an enabling environment, the transition process must start from below—by the people. In the Namibia workshop, participants identified four such models of transition—national conferences, popular revolutions, pact formations, and actions by the military—that have been used in African countries to remove dictators from office and to create or restore political pluralism.

In the last three years, national conferences, particularly in Francophone countries, have emerged as vehicles for representation, accountability, and consensus formation. These conferences have been convened as a result of citizen and elite pressures for public dialogue about the democratization process in countries such as Benin, Mali, Gabon, Zaire, Congo, Nigeria and Zambia. In addition, opposition groups in Cameroon, the Central African Republic, Guinea, and Côte d'Ivoire have called for national conferences in their countries. In some cases, national conferences have unceremoniously reduced or eliminated the powers of incumbent rulers. In Benin, for example, where the first national conference was held, Mathieu Kerekou broke down and wept as a national conference of ruling-party members and other leaders pronounced his repressive regime corrupt, incompetent, and illegal and even rejected an interim leadership role for him. In Togo, the national conference facilitated the emergence of the formerly clandestine opposition, although President Gnassingbé Eyadèma called out troops and declared the end of the transition effort on the final day of the national conference.

Participants underlined the importance of viewing national conferences as the beginning of an ongoing struggle toward democracy, rather than as an end. As such, national conferences should be regarded as part of a broad process resulting from a crisis situation. They would be best understood as opportunities to define and classify issues, establish accountability, and mobilize a broad cross-section of popular constituencies. Participants stressed that national conferences do not establish functioning democracies. Some participants in the Benin workshop noted that because the surprise effect of national conferences had vanished, it is unlikely that entrenched rulers would permit future national conferences to be held.

The common threads among successful national conferences were identified: the persistence of a crisis and agreement that it ought not continue; a prior change in government or government's explicit recognition that it must engage in dialogue; the recognition that all significant groups, including elites, participate, although no elections are held to determine those participants; and independent sponsorship. They indicated that national conferences have produced either constitutional review or a new constitution, have sometimes brought about a transitional government, and have led to elections.

After examining national conferences, participants also identified other alternative routes to democracy: popular revolution, as in the recent case of Ethiopia; action taken by the military, as in Mali and Sierra Leone; top-down concessions, as in Swaziland and Senegal; the top-down concession of self-imposed transitions to civil rule by the military in Nigeria; and pact formation, such as the Lancaster House Agreement, the Convention for a Democratic South Africa (CODESA), and negotiations in both Angola and Mozambique. Although each route was said to be loaded with problems, it was suggested that pact formations give the impression of a deal achieved undemocratically, thereby undercutting subsequent democratic legitimacy.

FUNDAMENTAL CHALLENGES TO
DEMOCRATIC TRANSITIONS

In the three workshops, participants identified fundamental challenges that will have to be confronted if the transition from authoritarian rule to democracy is to be consolidated in Africa.

The Cult of Personality

African politics has been described as a matter of personality, not programs, especially under single-party systems. In the Ethiopia workshop, one participant indicated that rulers have tended to encourage personality cults by having their portraits prominently and extensively displayed, assuming folk titles, and encouraging the use of slogans: "The idea of the president as the father of the nation, the big man, or being above the law is the prevailing political culture in Africa." Because of the high level of illiteracy in Africa, many politicians resort to such symbols in order to express their views to the masses. Another participant illustrated how this practice had manipulated the electorate: "During presidential campaigns in some rural areas in Benin, the people asked why they have to elect a new president when the old one is still alive." The issue of exploitation was further advanced by another participant, who stated: "In a country where there is 60-70 percent illiteracy, the campaign speeches by politicians, when translated to local languages, often are violations of conscience, because they provide only threads of information while deviously attacking the opposition party." In the transition to democracy, then, "the challenge is to break down the idea of the president being above the law and to stop looking at the other person who thinks differently as one's enemy."

Zero-Sum Politics

The winner-take-all practice in African political competition has been responsible for the elimination of an opposition as well as any political competition subsequent to elections. Participants in the three meetings proposed that bargaining become the new political culture in Africa: "The basic rule of the democracy game is that the winners do not forever dislodge the losers. It is important for the consolidation of democracy that losers believe in the system and think that they can get back into the game." They further suggested that the uncertainty of democracy through the ballot box—win today, lose tomorrow—had to be understood and accepted by any society in its transition to democracy. In the Namibia workshop, one participant described how former President Kenneth Kaunda of Zambia, after the election, went to the radio station to broadcast his resignation, and then personally removed the presidential flag from his car. The significance of Kaunda's action, which participants hoped other African leaders will emulate, is the public recognition that the president is subordinate to the people.

Participants argued that the notion of winner take all had heightened ethnic tensions, especially in countries with many ethnic groups. In such countries, it was suggested that there should be coalition building, bargaining, and a sharing of the rewards of power, which normally is what civilian politicians elsewhere in the world have to do in order to gain and keep power. As one participant put it: "The phenomenon of winner take all in competition is important in the context of ethnic problems. There must be bargaining, some give and take, because we cannot put the ethnic genie back into the bottle."

In one workshop, participants studied the electoral system of Mauritius, whose institutional arrangements recognize the losers as the loyal opposition. In Mauritius, because the "best losers" are reserved seats in parliament, they do not lose everything, a fact that, to some extent, reduces the zero-sum game. One participant argued that reserving seats in parliament for the opposition can hardly be regarded as a major innovation in the continent. However, participants stressed that the period of transition must include bargaining and essential compromises between state and society for the existent problems of political competition in Africa to be resolved. Participants agreed that there no longer should be a systematic throwing out of parties when they lose. In discussions of regional and local devolution of power, participants explored the relative advantages of these arrangements as a means of providing a power base for parties that lose at the national level.

The Military

Another key challenge is how to deal with one of the major contestants for political power in Africa: the military. Participants argued that, if the military is not transformed in the process of democratization, it would be difficult to have a dynamic civil society, because some actors would have an inordinate access to force: "The role of force in African politics must be examined. . . . There are difficulties in affecting democratic transitions in Africa when there are people who can and are playing the ethnic game of winner take all with guns. Where such force exists, the nightmare scenario of societal fragmentation into a series of armed warlords, such as in Liberia and Somalia, can emerge." However, as argued by another participant: "The problem with all militaries around the world, and not just Africa, is how to control them—not their access to force."

As one participant characterized it: "The plague of military intervention in politics by coups d'état has descended on Africa since independence. As a matter of fact, the first coup in sub-Saharan Africa occurred in Togo in 1963, that is, three years after most states became independent." There was agreement that African militaries do not respect the boundaries of the barracks, intervene in politics less out of altruistic motives than for a host of personal reasons, and arrogate to themselves the role of prescribing national goals and ideologies. Some thought the military threat is more severe today than in prior periods because the large-scale militarization that resulted from the cold war competition. Participants agreed that the arms race in Africa left tragic results. For example, prolonged periods of warfare and collapsing economies have left large numbers of young men with no skills, other than warfare, and few opportunities for civilian employment, even if they had the skills. Participants argued that the presence of formidable military forces in newly democratic or democratizing countries poses an ever-present temptation for intervention: "All issues become much more difficult to manage when some actors have access to force. The real issue we face, then, is violence, as potentially exercised by the military." Although much discussion focused on the military, participants did not agree on how best to confront the military threat in African politics. (Various nonconsensual suggestions that were advanced are discussed below.)

Managing Ethnicity

The ethnic variable, as participants labeled it, proved to be a contentious issue during the three workshops. There was a recognition that ethnic tensions in countries such as Nigeria, Uganda, Ghana, and Zimbabwe have led to violence and even civil wars. A widespread view evident among participants was that ignoring or suppressing ethnicity had failed in Africa.

Many participants advocated that ethnic groups be considered as integral parts of civil society and their strengths be recognized as an opportunity to solidify it. They argued that African countries currently undergoing transitions to democracy must find ways to deal with diversity among various ethnic groups, by managing ethnicity and recognizing the rights of individuals to promote their ethnicity. One participant commented: "Don't make tribalism disappear. Manage it, recognize the strength of it, but provide guarantees against the dreadful side of it, which can include patronage, expulsion, and massacres. In other words, tame it, because tribalism can be both satisfying and terrifying at the same time." Other participants, however, argued against the promotion of ethnicity, fearing that it might cause a redrawing of the map of Africa.

Participants identified two possible outcomes when leaders of ethnically diverse countries fail to address ethnicity during the transition period. First, a continued suppression of ethnic identities might lead to the emergence of open conflict, in which groups demand equal treatment and equal access to development. Second, in cases in which the state imposes an assimilation policy, depending on whether the needs of various elements are met adequately, there would be a distinct possibility that the groups would reject the imposed national identity. In this instance, either the assimilation policy would fail or a bargaining process wherein multiethnicity is recognized would begin. In addition, a number of participants voiced the opinion that multiethnic societies do not necessarily result in violence or exclusion of conflict, pointing out that "in most African societies, there is a fluid interaction among ethnic groups, through marriage and the marketplace."

The politicization of ethnic identities and the repression of one group by another were identified as primary sources of conflict. To promote ethnic coexistence, a bargaining process would have to recognize differences by striking a balance among groups. Participants advocated equal opportunities for all individuals, regardless of their ethnicity, and suggested also that the state transcend ethnic divisiveness and remain above all groups in society. Similarly, they argued that merit and professionalism, rather than ethnicity, should be the primary criteria for promotion to national offices or to the civil service. Because some groups had been advantaged at the expense of others, the sense among participants was that equal access to education, the recognition of ethnic languages, and some interim affirmative action would be needed to ensure that hitherto disadvantaged groups and regions would not be excluded from meaningful participation in society. Although such measures might reduce the political salience of ethnicity, participants acknowledged they would be difficult to achieve, particularly in view of the cultural traditions that virtually demand preferential treatment of one's own ethnic group in the access to public resources. Although there was agreement on democracy providing a framework within which ethnic groups could negotiate and live together, some argued that the strength of ethnicity had to be recognized as an opportunity to build civil society, while others remained to be convinced that promoting ethnicity is not an obstacle to democratization.

The Role of Women

The crucial role of women in the democratization process was acknowledged by participants in the three workshops. Some suggested that the democratic wave has not adequately addressed the expectations of women, especially rural women at the grass roots level. They indicated that women were not consulted in the governance or transition process, despite their constituting the majority of the labor force. One participant observed: "Women make up at least 50 percent of the population in Africa and are active at the grass roots level. We need to help make other women aware of the democratization trend. . . . We face illiteracy, so we must educate women, but also lessen their burden, give them time to think, to participate in new political conditions, through family planning, child care, welfare, and income-generating activities. If they had economic independence and used family planning, they could develop themselves and be empowered, thus playing an important role in organizations."

The subordination of women in Africa, argued the participants, has strong historical roots that have been reinforced by contemporary legal codes. In countries subject to Roman-Dutch law, such as South Africa and Namibia, gender inequality is explicitly codified in law. In other countries, women may have nominal rights, but still face legal discrimination. As a participant from Zambia noted, "the National Women's Lobby Group of Zambia has identified 99 laws that discriminate against women—and these provisions are in the process of being repealed." Most participants held that women's rights would not be achieved by granting decrees of equality but through a socialization process, whereby legal rights would be recognized and entrenched in order to promote women's interests and heighten their participation. Nevertheless, participants did recognize that changes in African legal codes would constitute an affirmation by society that women and men are equal human beings. Participants further argued that the entire democratization process should be accompanied by a positive campaign of empowerment and access to the legal system, emphasizing the rights of women, children, and the poor. Participants noted that the unequal and often debased position of women in African societies is a major obstacle to democratization: "Women are overwhelmed by problems of daily survival. . . . In addition to their economic marginalization, their role is further constrained by cultural, religious, and ideological orientation. . . . Once they begin to understand and exercise their power, they will play a significant role. Because of women's proximity to the oppressive power of the state and as a primary socializing agent, their role is crucial to any society aspiring to democracy."

Although subsequent discussions focused on decreasing the gender gap in social relations, participants also suggested an examination of linguistic and social barriers, particularly the disrespectful way in which women are addressed and language that portrays them as lesser beings. One person commented: "Women should be emancipated from economic dependence and domestic slavery. . . . Some programs of affirmative action might be appropriate, such as reserving seats for women in local and regional organizations, as is done in Uganda." Although affirmative action was encouraged by some, others stressed that democratic rights should be universal, because affirmative action, employed in excess by creating separate rights for women, could create more inequality. Nevertheless, there was agreement on the need to educate both men and women on gender issues relating to democratization.

Some participants advocated examining the cultural and religious limitations on the roles women can play, because it will take time and socialization to overcome such constraints. Yet a number of women cautioned against being prescriptive or assuming that a particular religious environment precludes possibilities. Specifically, the African women participants advocated providing women with economic opportunities that would enable them to find their own way of participating. Still others believed that the gender issue should be pursued, but with no illusions, asking: "Are we talking about feminism or of the participation of women as members of society in order to enable their contribution to the democratic process, which eventually could result in gender equality?" The discussions pointed out that democratic rights are basic rights that should include women. It was stressed that one of the main obstacles is African men, whose traditional roles give them privileges they are not willing to relinquish.

In short, the three workshops affirmed the crucial nature of the role played by women to any modern society aspiring to democracy. It is critical for this role to be understood during the transition process, when women must have opportunities to have their own voices heard.

PRECONDITIONS FOR DEMOCRACY

One significant ingredient of democratic transitions identified in the meetings was the creation of an enabling environment, which would permit citizens to live in accordance with their beliefs and rights without obstruction from government. One view was that the proper role of government is to create an enabling environment in which traditions and values of the constitution will be able to take root and where rights and duties are set out.

In this process, the separation of powers must be facilitated. Government must allow institutions to work and must allow citizens to exercise their rights, to live in accordance with their religious beliefs and cultural values, without interference. There was no clear agreement, however, on whether government should be responsible for the creation of such an environment.

Other participants suggested that societal organizations such as nongovernmental organizations and private voluntary organizations should assume primary responsibility for creating an enabling environment. In some cases, it was pointed out, the societal organizations, which had gone underground because they were suppressed by government, must be allowed to resurface in order to contribute to the creation of such an environment. They noted: "The expectation that government will create an enabling atmosphere is misleading, as it puts the imperative on the state. The African state actually has pushed out societal needs and created an environment for itself. Societal groups must strive to ensure that an enabling environment is created. The job should not be left to government, but government should allow the society room to operate."

Regardless of whether societal organizations or the state assumes the responsibility for creating or facilitating an enabling environment, participants identified certain prerequisites for an enabling environment, which include a legal order based on human rights, societal awareness of the instrumental and intrinsic values of democracy, a competent state, a committed minority, courage, and a culture of tolerance.

Legal Order and Basic Rights

In many precolonial African countries, despotism was the rule, and societies in which basic rights could be asserted before the seventeenth century were few and far between. Such rights did exist, however. Although hardly a reflection of the existence of civil rights or of a democratic order, they set the boundaries between rulers and subjects, guaranteeing that individuals are protected from despotic control of those exercising state powers. For example, in many African societies, rulers who abused power or acted *ultra vires* (outside the traditionally prescribed rules governing the conduct of rulers) could be and were frequently removed from office by various means. In contemporary Africa, the state's monopoly of power and its disregard for individual liberties and freedoms generally have led to an erosion or, in some cases, complete absence of government legitimacy.

Because it is commonly understood that human rights constitute the most important concerns of human society and civilization, participants agreed that popular participation and a legal order without guarantees for individual rights would not contribute to the establishment of democracy. Identifying the state as the major violator of human rights in Africa, participants suggested that institutions that are respected by the people and a system that has the legal authority to regulate the state would have to be invented: "Liberal democracies respect the rights of the individual. Freedoms of the individual are critical to African participation and thus progress toward democracy." Notably, a number of African lawyers and judges at the workshops stressed that "one should proceed with caution regarding collective rights." Those that "addressed cultural rights and the freedom of assembly," they argued, "have a valid function, but group rights should not override individual rights."

Some participants suggested that one means of strengthening human rights in this second liberation of Africa would be to publicize and explain the Universal Declaration of Human Rights. Inasmuch as the fundamental rights and freedoms written into African constitutions were modeled after the Universal Declaration, participants said that the international standards of human rights applied to all, whether or not a particular country had ratified additional human rights instruments. Such discussion also turned to questions concerning the protection and enforcement of individual rights, wherein civic education and legal aid were proposed as means of encouraging people to know and defend their rights. On a practical level, there were many ideas about how to communicate concepts of freedom and political rights to largely illiterate peasant communities (discussed below).

The discussions of human rights and safeguards led to the issue of a normative order in society when individuals start to question the legitimacy of their rulers. One participant indicated that the basis of legitimacy could be identified from inputs and outputs: "Does government have the right to rule; was it elected? Is government ruling rightly, delivering the goods it promised the people?" In this context, reciprocity between state and society—between governors and the governed, between those who exercise political leadership in society and those who are led, between those who exercise authority and those who are the subjects of this authority—was identified as a significant element of democracy. Democracy requires that those who have authority use it for the public good, in a democratic system of government that begins by recognizing all members of society are equal. Participants agreed that people should have equal say and equal participation in the affairs of government and decision making in society, because, in the final analysis, government exists to serve the people; the people do not exist to serve government. In other words, governments must enhance individual rights and not stifle their existence.

In demarcating new boundaries between African states and societies, it was suggested by some that the rule of law needs to be established. One participant commented: "When there is an open process, but no legal context, the battle between the government and opposition forces has no legal reference. This is the case now in Zaire." Other participants brought the debate full circle by advocating that human rights must be at the center of a new legal order: "Repressive laws on African statute books against personal liberty and habeas corpus are decrees euphemistically called laws. Such laws must be removed from the statute books."

Values of Democracy

During the transition toward Africa's second independence, individuals are saying that they want to determine their own future. Yet, in order to help the transition process along, participants argued that society as a whole needs to be aware of the instrumental and intrinsic values of democracy.

In most African countries, participants recognized that a tremendous amount of information does not circulate beyond a small portion of the urban population, owing to illiteracy, language barriers, and costs. Because, as one person commented, the "individual ignorance of personal rights and understanding of what democracy means has encouraged authoritarianism in Africa," some participants wanted political education at the grass roots level about democracy. For example, someone suggested that local student councils could help teach students about real ideas and practices in democratic management. Others indicated practical lessons in democracy at the grass roots level could be learned by serving in local government—inasmuch as there tends to be greater accountability where government is in close proximity to people.

Other participants, however, took exception to the view of educating only the masses, suggesting that politicians should be educated about human rights and respect for the constitution. As one put it: "Masses do have a wisdom that intellectuals should learn. If we want genuine democracy, the participation of the masses has to be sought by politicians, and not bought by manipulators. . . . Politicians should try to understand what the masses know, because they sometimes lack the ability to articulate their interests and grievances. This way their contribution in society is ensured."

There was clear agreement among participants in the three workshops that some form of resocialization to promote political culture had to be undertaken, as "negative values had been inculcated for so long." One cannot legislate political culture. One must look at the issues—what have been the costs, and what do we need to move away from? In a moving plea in the Ethiopia workshop, one participant suggested that "if we are to recognize that our societies are heterogenous, maybe we can overcome the fear of transition with a culture of tolerance. . . . How to reach it? Through mutual recognition, consensus, compromise, not fear." It was then pointed out that education would be crucial to the development of a culture of tolerance, which, it was hoped, would contribute immensely to the creation of an enabling environment for democracy: "We must encourage citizens to learn the habits of civil disobedience on a massive scale. . . . We must encourage people to go out and demonstrate, to show their opinion regarding issues, because we must eliminate the culture of fear."

Competent State

The current crisis in Africa, participants pointed out, is a crisis of the state and its incompetence in development. In the three workshops, the need for an alternative view of the state was identified—a state capable of assisting in the transition from authoritarian rule to democracy. Citing the government's breakdown of authority, lack of legitimacy, and unwillingness to bargain, a number of participants described African states as "lame leviathans." Similarly, another participant indicated that the problem was that African governments are not governing and, in their present makeup, do not have the capacity to do so: "The repressive nature of the African state, which is suspended over society without effective linkages to the community it is supposed to govern, reveals its weak character." One participant further argued that "the weakness of African states has been exposed by the fact that they are addicted to foreign aid. They have perfected the art of begging and dialogue with the donor community rather than with their own people." Another suggested, "there has to be a reassessment of the relationship between state and society for democracy to succeed in Africa." And another said "through reciprocal bargaining between state and society, a new set of legitimate and predictable relations could be developed. In this manner, civil society would emerge as a counter to the state." It was generally agreed that state power needed to be checked, particularly because "civil society largely had fallen prey to the state or had been coopted by it." In the future, the state "must induce its constituents and not pursue them." In a phrase coined by one of the participants in Ethiopia and later endorsed all the participants, she maintained, "the state must socialize rather than mobilize." In other words, democracy depends on governments that grow out of their own societies. The attempt by many African governments since independence to mold societies into an image shaped by their own governments is doomed to failure. The same, after all, has been true of former Soviet Union.

In postcolonial society, the state had become the "desired political kingdom." The process of evolution from colonial rule to authoritarian rule, in one participant's words, "has been like playing fast forward on a tape. . . . In this context of accelerated state formation, the autonomous needs of civil society were considered impediments that needed to be broken down." There was some agreement on the imperative to create an effective public arena, as the state had been "privatized" by governing elites. Several participants, however, objected to the view that the state crisis in Africa was the primary problem in all countries, indicating that "the problem is not whether the state is competent or incompetent, but how to prevent the state from becoming too predatory, or from turning itself into an instrument of extraordinary power." The question was raised as to how to get individuals to trust the state again after decades of viewing it as a predator rather than a facilitator: "Because the state in Africa is currently the number one owner, there ought to be a socialization of ownership. In this context, privatization and the need to reduce the centrality of the state to economic means are essential." Finally, in the transition from authoritarian rule to democracy, there was agreement that "one should neither destroy the state or leave it to wither away, but should help the state find its proper role." In other words, democracy is not the same as anarchy, and it can be achieved only within an effective state structure; ultimately, a working democracy will create a stronger state—because it is legitimate and accountable—rather than a weaker one.

ROLE OF CIVIL SOCIETY

The significance of a lively civil society in the transition to democracy was emphasized in the three workshops. The participants took some comfort in noting that one reason that Africa did not crumble into total absolutism was because civil society managed to survive, providing a mode of expression against authoritarianism, despite systematic efforts by the state to destroy it.

A participant pointed out that civil society in Africa has been shaped by its relationship not only to the state, but also with other units in society. A recurring pattern has been the retreat of organizations of civil society into discrete arenas. The participant identified three types: a "submerged society," in which needs are met through patronage networks; a "defiant society," in which state authority is openly ignored by gangs and bandits in what may be described as a Hobbesian state of nature; and a "radicalized society," mobilized to replace the existing state, which includes such disparate groups as national liberation groups and religious fundamentalists. In all three cases, the legitimacy of the state is challenged. In the workshop discussions, it was suggested that the opening up of political space for civil society was crucial to the success of democratization.

One consequence of civil institutions operating in an underground mode is that few of them are broadly inclusive of diverse elements in the community, and so they are generally unable to bridge ethnic, linguistic, or other divisions in the community. Consequently, it was suggested that the public put pressure on the state to open up political space for civil society and that efforts be made to promote a society that includes broad cross-sections of the community. The basis of civil society is common interests, independent of the state, through which people can organize themselves and relate to one another on a national basis. The major institutions through which civil society has reemerged in modern Africa are religious organizations, notably the churches; trade unions; and professionals—lawyers, journalists, academics.

Participants identified varying perceptions of the state in African countries. In Tanzania, for example, as pointed out by one participant, the state is referred to as "big daddy." In Zaire, the state is associated with harassment. In other countries, the state is linked with statism, taking over everything, including how one ought to think. There was agreement that it would be incumbent upon civil society to promote socialization by moving people away from thinking about the state and encouraging them to think what they want without fear. One participant observed: "Under Jomo Kenyatta, there was an entrenchment of democratic institutions; but, under Daniel arap Moi, there has been a concentrated destruction of institutions. Happily, the people of Kenya are beginning to ask what went wrong."

According to a number of participants, the extreme frailty of civil society in some African countries has left the citizenry with only the voice and exit options. Using the voice option, some individuals and organizations confronted the state and questioned state interference in their personal and family lives. In so doing, they had to contend with constant harassment from the state, which often led to violations of their individual and collective rights. The exit option has become common in countries such as Ethiopia, Sudan, and Rwanda, where there was a forced exodus of outspoken individuals or organizations. It was argued that Africans have been conditioned to exercise the exit option because the state has been regarded as a hostile force. In order to build an animated civil society, participants advocated recapturing the population that has distanced itself from authoritarian power.

In southern Africa, for example, civil society has been exposed, restricted by law, or formed in secret, but it has maintained a role in articulating public values, while resisting state control. In single-party states, such as Tanzania, independent civic groups generally were regarded as subversive and therefore had been wiped out over 28 years. In several countries, including Madagascar, Zambia, and South Africa, organizations that taught elements of civic culture initially were established secretly by concerned citizens and emerged only when they gained sufficient strength and perceived a political opening. Churches united in ecumenical movements, however, have been able to resist state control, playing a major role in articulating public values in much of the southern Africa region. They also have served to integrate ethnically diverse regions.

In the three workshops, the capacity of institutions of civil society to organize upward in public life was linked to the crisis of the African state and to the ability of entrenched rulers to resist change. In Malawi, for example, public organizations have not been able to operate openly until recently. In Zambia, by contrast, the catastrophic economic record of the government of Kenneth Kaunda led to a crisis of authority, which prompted public institutions to assert themselves. In South Africa, the churches and popular movements associated with the United Democratic Front were able to take advantage of the crisis of apartheid, which was revealed by the succession of F.W. de Klerk. In these openings, participants noted that civil society had to provide new alternatives as well as leaders whose authority was rooted in their own record. Some cited President Frederick Chiluba of Zambia, whose experience in the trade union movement, political detention, and refusal to be coopted by the previous regime bears striking resemblances to President Lech Walesa of Poland. It was also pointed out that a new and vibrant local leadership had arisen in South Africa.

Several suggestions were put forward by participants about how to build civil society in order to enhance democratic culture. One participant proposed that an active citizenry together with nongovernmental organization, which play a role independent of government or political parties, could take center stage in public life: "The public must fully participate in the affairs of state, with the state protecting their rights to be recognized. In this context, the value of the role of citizens and civil society is to organize and articulate the interests of local communities and the grass roots to the highest levels—even bringing about the change of laws—by serving as effective pressure groups." Another observation was that "where democracy has taken root, there have been associations and groupings. These groups have acted as pressure points to democratize government. For the most part, these groups have acted in isolation. Concerted action would have made them more powerful. There ought to be more coordination of action among groups. Yet, groups must be autonomous organizationally and financially, so as not to be coopted during the process. In this manner, democratic culture will emerge in civil society." Some participants cautioned however, that state coercion over the public to participate is equally dangerous to the establishment of democracy.

Although the formation of civil society was considered a positive process in democratization, several participants cautioned that it happens only when people take risks, investing their time, energies, and lives. In the words of one participant, "many governments are not willing to create an enabling environment. I have no illusions about this. But, by standing up, individuals can insist and force government to create a space." In the workshop in Ethiopia, some indicated that an enlightened minority of society would have special responsibilities, which "would be discharged properly only when there are proper linkages extending downward and broadened to benefit the community at large."

It was also suggested that one builds civil society by developing a culture in communities, utilizing organizations that teach people public culture. One participant advocated not relying on the "father state" to engineer the process: "National commissions set up by the state in some countries to help build civil societies can be useful, but should not be a reason for civil society not to assume its responsibilities. The community must keep the culture of resistance alive and question authority. Maybe we Africans have resigned from our responsibilities, as we rely on Amnesty International and other international organizations to do our work for us. Are we prepared to start something on a pan-African basis to be a moral force?"

In sum, a strong civil society in Africa was believed to be an essential prerequisite for successful transitions to democracy. Participants thought that the increasing presence of civic groups would be good indicators of where a government stands regarding the rights of expression and assembly as well as democracy in general.

Committed Minority

It has been argued by some scholars that democracy is built only around democrats. As one participant put it, "Without a sizable minority of democrats and constitutionalists, the quest for democracy in Africa would come to naught" if the impetus is to be provided only by the state. Another participant spoke of citizen responsibility and emphasized the role of academics and intellectuals, arguing that "the enlightened sectors of society have to assume their responsibilities with humility and patriotism. They must initiate a constituent group in favor of constitutionalism and democracy. These individuals must be committed to liberty and justice, irrespective of the machine gun, acting as catalysts for society as a whole."

Some participants raised questions regarding the assertion that intellectuals should lead the struggle toward democracy. One commented: "Intellectuals in some African countries have become organic means of power by giving dictatorial regimes legitimacy. Because they have been provided material benefits by the dictators, intellectuals often have propounded theories to justify policies by the rulers, thereby preparing the grave for democracy." Several universities were cited as examples of how intellectuals cannot educate people effectively on democracy, because they lack popular legitimacy from having been supported by dictators over the years.

Some participants argued that a middle class might be a prerequisite for democracy. This suggestion was qualified by others, who pointed out that "it is not the middle class, as such, that promotes liberal democracy, but a section of the middle class that is committed to democracy." According to them, a sizable minority of supporters in the middle class might be necessary for the emergence of liberal democracy. Thus, the critical issue in the democratization process which should be addressed, is how to build democracy in the absence of democrats.

Courage

The word *courage* often was employed in the three workshops. "Challenging the status quo, especially in African countries, does require courage because it is difficult to ask people to take big risks. . . . There is importance in surmounting the culture of fear, as well as self-empowerment among people who take risks and find tremendous power in doing so. Moreover, government can't cope when people do this." It also was suggested by one participant that, "although citizens in African countries have not acted in concert in pushing for democracy, people were not to underestimate the powers of citizenry, who should seek academics' advice to help with strategy."

In conclusion, it is important to qualify that, although the nature of the transition to democracy varies from country to country, there have been common sociological, political, and economic constraints on developing democratic societies throughout Africa. Some of these constraints include inefficient bureaucracies, fragile institutions, economies in serious trouble, and an undemocratic political culture wherein people live in fear with little trust or pride in government. Some participants also proposed that the "normative and structural aspects need to be examined, because the African state of today is both a product of colonial structures and its own indigenous forms. In this context, one also cannot ignore scarcity in Africa, particularly because economic and political resources have been distributed in a personal, not egalitarian manner."

Whatever democratic progress has been accomplished in Africa by the early 1990s still is largely structural or constitutional. The process of transition to democracy in Africa will probably be long and painful. Much success will depend on the quality of leadership at all levels operating during the transitional phase to democracy.

3

Democracy and Governance in Africa

Africa's continuing reliance on foreign aid has increased the opportunities for bilateral and multilateral aid agencies to influence policy making in the region. The major donors have been meeting frequently in order to discuss development and debt problems and to devise aid strategies for African governments. In turn, foreign aid has increasingly been linked to a set of prescriptions for changes in both economic and political policies pursued by African governments. The so-called new world order also has had significant effects on African governments. As the influence and interest of the Soviet Union in Africa declined (and later collapsed with its demise), Western states and the organizations they influence gained considerably greater leverage over African governments, surpassing the general client-dependent relationship of the 1970s and 1980s.

In the 1980s, the international financial institutions announced that the implementation of structural adjustment and economic stabilization programs would be conditions for their assistance to African governments. The World Bank, the International Monetary Fund, and the U.S. Agency for International Development took the lead in demanding policy changes, such as currency devaluation, removal of subsidies for public services, reduction of state intervention in agricultural pricing and marketing, greater concern to the development needs of rural areas, privatization of parastatal bodies, and reduction in the size and cost of the public sector.

In the early 1990s, donors began to show interest in promoting political change in addition to economic reforms. Democratic political reforms were emphasized as key factors in the determination of future economic assistance for Africa. The Development Advisory Committee of the Organization for Economic Cooperation and Development is on record in support of "participatory development," which includes democratization, improved governance, and human rights. The condition that political reforms be undertaken is now attached at least rhetorically to almost all Western aid. Actual donor practices vary: France proposes greater liberty and democracy, Great Britain recommends good government, the United States focuses on good governance, Japan talks about linking aid to reductions in military expenditures. Yet, regardless of the approach, there is increasingly strong agreement among donors that political reforms in Africa must result in reduced corruption and more financial accountability, better observance of human rights, independent media and an independent judiciary, participatory politics, and a liberalized market economy in order to move closer to the ultimate goal of meaningful economic growth and development.

GOVERNANCE AND AFRICAN POLITICS

Improved governance, which appears to be the common donor requirement for the release of both bilateral and multilateral aid to African countries, has been defined diversely among different observers and actors concerned with development in Africa. The World Bank, for example, defines governance as "the manner in which power is exercised in the management of a country's economic and social resources for development."[5] The World Bank's definition further emphasizes its concern with efficiency and the capacity of state institutions beyond the public sector to the rules and institutions that create a predictable and transparent framework for the conduct of public and private business, as well as accountability for economic and financial performance.

A number of political scientists participating in the Namibia workshop found it necessary to point out that the concepts of democracy and governance were interrelated, but were not the same. They indicated that "good governance entails the efficient and effective reciprocity between rulers and the ruled, with it incumbent upon government to be responsive. . . . Majoritarian democracy, on the other hand, entailed a broad consensus on values and procedures, the participation in the selection of ruling elites, and the accountability of leadership to the electorate. . . . Both concepts were related to processes in society within the context of reciprocity." Although partici-

---

[5] Managing Development: The Governance Dimension. Discussion paper, World Bank, 1991.

pants at the other workshops did not define the term *governance*, a number of participants thought the World Bank's definition and discussions of good governance were too narrow. Still, there was agreement in the meetings that African governments are deeply in need of governance reforms.

In the Namibia meeting, one participant was of the opinion that the argument that all of Africa has practiced bad governance "is not an accurate statement. . . . In reality, there are few Mobutu Sese Sekos. Most African governments have been in difficult situations and they have opted for the easy way out. Foreign governments did not insist on good governance, either. Even when policies failed, assistance kept coming. Only recently have donors been raising the governance issue, linking it to assistance in order to ensure that the economy and politics be liberalized. Increasingly, Africans are saying that such conditions should be tied to policy performance, but not to a particular blueprint for democracy. Africans should design their own approach to democracy, make a good-faith effort to govern well and to have programs work in an efficient manner, and strive for the development of a culture of democracy between the rulers and the ruled. . . . Perhaps improved governance will take hold before democracy. Africa is liberalizing, but it will take time, and one must be prepared to persevere for a long haul."

Participants identified the major reasons for poor governance and "bad" politics in African countries as the personalized nature of rule, the failure of the state to advance and protect human rights, the tendency of individuals to withdraw from politics, and the extreme centralization of power in the hands of few people. It was pointed out also that democracy in Africa has been badly hindered by the state's control of the economy; this has meant that the only way to get rich has been through political office, intensifying the problem of corruption, and inducing leaders to cling to political power. This has been disastrous for the economies in African countries. Thus, economic liberalization, empowering ordinary producers, may well be an aid to political democracy.

Furthermore, in most African countries, the small number of individuals with power have managed to erode any semblance of accountability, legitimacy, democracy, and justice, which has been a basis of considerable disappointment to the planners, economists and policy makers who want African governments to introduce a reasonable and collective attack on poverty, disease, illiteracy, and other challenges to development. In the deliberations, certain desperately needed elements of good governance were identified, including popular participation in governance, accountability and transparency, the elimination of corruption, the protection of freedom of information and human rights, and the decentralization and devolution of power.

POPULAR PARTICIPATION

Africans have acknowledged that development must be revamped by a democratic approach employing the energy and devotion of African people—who alone can make development sustainable. This recognition emerged from the Arusha Conference "Putting the People First" of February 1990, convened under the auspices of the United Nations Economic Commission for Africa and attended by over 500 delegations representing grass roots organizations, nongovernmental organizations, United Nations agencies, and governments. The *African Charter for Popular Participation in Development and Transformation*, which was adopted by the plenary, holds that the absence of democracy is a principal reason for the persistent development challenges facing Africa:[6]

> We affirm that nations cannot be built without the popular support and full participation of the people, nor can the economic crisis be resolved and the human and economic conditions improved without the full and effective contribution, creativity, and popular enthusiasm of the vast majority of the people. After all, it is to the people that the very benefits of development should and must accrue. We are convinced that neither can Africa's perpetual economic crisis be overcome, nor can a bright future for Africa and its people see the light of day unless the structures, pattern, and political context of the process of socioeconomic development are appropriately altered.

In the three workshops, the importance of popular participation in building democratic society likewise was underscored: "The significance of ordinary people having power is important in any society moving toward democracy. When one examines existing democratic societies, one realizes they have succeeded primarily because they have involved people to help make it work. . . . Also, they have empowered those engaged in democratic projects. In short, they have succeeded by giving voice to those who have been voiceless."

In discussions on the importance of popular participation in democracy, participants suggested distinguishing between "true" and "false" participation. "False participation," argued some participants, "has been used by many African governments to project an appearance of support for government policies, but actually tends to promote the cult of personality and to stifle individual and local initiatives. As such, critics of the government either are intimidated or absorbed. "True participation," in contrast, "con-

---

[6] *African Charter for Popular Participation in Development Transformation (Arusha 1990)* International Conference on Popular Participation in the Recovery and Development Process in Africa, 12-16 February.

stantly must seek to present the views of individuals from the grass roots level." It was noted that, in practice, true participation is difficult to maintain because the movement for participation can be "hijacked by opportunist politicians who use it to project themselves into influential positions." Although participants noted that external donors sometimes play an important role in empowering local communities, as in South Africa, they cautioned that the grass roots communities need to guard against falling into a culture of dependence: "Donors, too, may find themselves supporting the most articulate elements in African societies, who may be relatively wealthy and well educated, but not necessarily representative. Foreign nongovernmental organizations also tend to work with governments and may be used by them in order to promote government patronage."

Furthermore, participants noted that the legal restrictions on participation remaining in some countries would have to be removed. For example, it was noted that "measures that require the registration of civic associations, such as trade unions or student movements, have been used by governments to dissolve associations on petty pretexts." But participants agreed that "ultimately, it is up to individuals to assert their right to participate, if necessary defying or circumventing official restrictions." Participants also went a step further, advocating that internal accountability be maintained within civic associations in order to ensure that spokespersons represent their constituents. It also was suggested that civic associations become institutionalized and begin to support one another. Explicit measures to this end have been taken in Zambia since the recent presidential elections. One participant also pointed out that nongovernmental organizations in Namibia were inculcating a sense of participatory democracy in their projects, including in the schools.

In discussing the relationship between participation and efficiency, the question of what is meant by efficiency was raised. Participants suggested that "a technocratic approach to efficiency takes political issues out of the hands of the people and stifles participation. One classic example of this approach has been the imposition of structural adjustment programs, under which the entire management of the economy is removed from the realm of participatory politics. If, on the other hand, the efficiency of the government is to be measured by its ability to meet the needs of its people, then a high level of participation can only promote this end." Supporting what the World Bank has called "consultation of the project beneficiaries," one participant asked whether "the economic reforms of 1986 in Tanzania couldn't have taken place differently if there had been broad-based public discussions in which the public was allowed to take part. . . . Discussions could have helped people to be prepared for the impact of reforms. . . . In this manner, perhaps the reforms even could have been softened." A number of participants further pondered whether government has the right to choose policies that affect people's livelihood without consulting them. If efficiency is measured by the government's ability to meet the needs of its people, they suggest, then "the first task of government is to make sure citizens' lives improve on a daily basis, because if citizens do not see improvement, their enthusiasm for supporting government policies wanes."

There was overwhelming agreement among participants that poor governance has adversely affected the efficient use of economic and social resources for development in African countries. The misuse or diversion of assistance and domestic funds by corrupt officials, which was tolerated during the cold war to receive support in the international system, is being replaced by a new emphasis on good governance. In the past, said a number of participants, "aid appeared to be driven by certain political factors without a congruence of interests between givers and receivers." The trend with donor assistance is to channel money through nongovernmental organizations, other private voluntary organizations, and even the private sector rather than to governments. Among some participants, the assumption is that such groups can act as watchdogs, serving as the best deliverers of assistance; a number of participants did not agree, arguing that newly democratic governments should receive and channel such aid.

NEED FOR ACCOUNTABILITY AND TRANSPARENCY

In any society, holding citizens responsible for their actions, in public service and the private sector, is significant to ensure some level of accountability. With regard to public officials, participants pointed out that mechanisms must be devised to hold leaders responsible when they use public resources in ways that society considers unacceptable. To that end, they noted that any public accountability system should include periodic competition and a clear set of rules and expectations. Participants emphasized the notion that the principle of accountability, essential to democracy, requires exposing the truth, with stated and enforced consequences for violating the rules, without exception, even for those in power. The lack of accountability in Africa has led to the gross misuse of public resources. For example, single-party systems in Africa do not allow for much in the way of accountability. The effect has been rampant corruption and the deterioration of socioeconomic conditions—an indication that people in Africa were governed without being able to control their governors. One participant argued: "Besides financial and economic accountability, there is also a need for electoral accountability, for the right to recall representatives if they do not deliver on their promises and don't govern well."

International financial institutions and bilateral donors have addressed their expectations of both economic and financial accountability from African countries. The economic objectives of public accountability sought by the World Bank, for example, include congruence between public policy and actual implementation and the efficient allocation and use of public resources. This not only requires systems of financial accountability, but also the capacity and willingness to monitor the overall economic performance of the government.

Another challenge discussed under the rubric of good governance was to achieve transparency in government transactions. In most African countries, participants noted that it is difficult to find functioning establishments in which government accounts, external procurement procedures, and central bank operations are discussed objectively: "In examining the way the economy is managed and the structure of relationships between government and society, there is need for greater transparency. The state must be deprivatized [from domination by the few] and a public arena must be created where there would be room for argument and discussions based on what is good for the entire society. Things should be argued in public terms so that everyone can participate on an equal basis." Thus, participants argued that transparent decision making might serve as a safeguard against corruption, waste, and the abuse of executive authority.

Several participants pointed out that government should not conceal information from its citizens. A number of suggestions were put forward by participants regarding the ways in which transparency might be achieved in Africa. These included freedom of the press, donors' insistence that governments make their ledgers and gazettes public knowledge, requiring declarations of assets from public officials, exposing and confronting corruption, and accountability from below. Some participants also raised the question of whether donors genuinely verify democratic conditions in recipient countries, such as Liberia and Kenya. In the case of Liberia, participants suggested U.S. assistance was given despite documented evidence of widespread human rights violations and the inability to implement fiscal accountability because of domestic fighting between indigenous factions. With regard to Kenya, participants pointed out the inconsistency in application of the good government policy advocated by the British, compared with other bilateral donors. Despite Daniel arap Moi's initial reluctance to yield to the demands for multiparty politics, Kenya received substantial British investment and was defended by both Foreign Minister Douglas Hurd and Aid Minister Lynda Chalker as having a good human rights record. One participant argued, "Perhaps democracy is being used as a legitimation of intervention. . . . There is a need for transparency in the advice donors give to African governments. When projects [that have been agreed on behind closed doors] fail, the onus is put on African governments." Most participants were of the opinion that this practice was unjustified, especially because the public officials representing African governments in such negotiations often lack credibility and legitimacy.

In this regard, it was suggested that donors also need to apply governance reforms to the way they conduct business. One participant stated, "Having worked for several aid agencies, I will add that the donors need to undertake governance reforms. I hope that the progressive and democratic forces in Africa both during and after the transition will demand those reforms of the donors. For example, demand the publication of confidential reports of the World Bank and International Monetary Fund. . . . They are confidential only in lessening the level of accountability of these agencies to populations and opposition. . . . I think there should be much more transparency in the policy-making process, especially during structural adjustment negotiations. . . . That lack of transparency has satisfied only the donors and the governments, and it will be interesting to see, after the transition, whether newly democratic governments will open up this process to the press, and I think they should, because it will much improve the structural adjustment process." In short, participants demanded more openness regarding the dialogue and agreements reached between African governments and the donor community.

CORRUPTION

The issue of corruption was identified as posing a profound threat to all systems of government. In most African countries, corruption constitutes an important means by which individual wants and needs, especially in patronage-ridden personal regimes, can be satisfied. Although corruption is a general problem for all governments, governments of developing countries tend to exhibit the problem in a particularly noteworthy way. In countries such as Nigeria, Ghana, Sierra Leone, Zaire, and the Central African Republic, corruption is so extensive that it is viewed as a way of life. Making or receiving bribes in most African countries is considered a practical tactic to look after one's needs and interests, achieving incomes and security far greater than provided by one's monthly salary. Because of an absence of effective structures with autonomy and strength to check corruption, the governing elites of most African countries have engaged in high and sometimes egregious levels of corruption, increasingly diverting state resources for personal gain. In Zaire, for example, one participant mentioned that corruption has been termed a structural fact, with as much as 60 percent of the annual budget misappropriated by the governing elite.

Foreign aid, noted the participants, although designed to contribute to development, also has served as an alternative source of wealth for corrupt elites. One commented: "While many African leaders have become rent-seeking and corrupt, there is a corruptor and a corruptee." A number of participants pointed out how some of those providing assistance collude with corrupt leaders, promoting the syndrome of capital flight. They then suggested that donors cease dealing with leaders who have amassed extraordinary fortunes by transferring their country's foreign exchange into private accounts overseas. It was also pointed out that, to the extent that government has been immersed in patron-client relations and in cases in which state office is granted as a means to amass personal wealth, corruption has increased in scale and proportion.

One significant suggestion advanced by participants in both the Benin and Namibia workshops was that public monies siphoned off by corrupt leaders and public officials and deposited in the West must be returned. They made a plea for donors to suggest steps that African countries could take that might help retrieve the stolen money deposited in foreign accounts by these public officials. One participant stated, "Stolen monies do not belong to the few individuals who perpetrated the thefts. . . . The people of African countries were robbed. If donors were to try to help get this money back, it maybe would contribute to democracy and democratization." As an example that repatriation is possible, one of the Zambian participants stated that Zambians had been assured by British Prime Minister John Major that such public funds deposited in the United Kingdom would be returned.

Although participants acknowledged that corruption in Africa emanated from the lack of democracy and accountability, they emphasized that corruption is not unique to Africa and also may be found in liberal democratic systems. Consequently, they were of the opinion that the real issue is the absence of institutions capable of tackling corruption. As one participant argued, "With regard to corruption and stolen money, my own advice is to let sleeping dogs lie and engage ourselves more in how to create institutions that will help make a repeat performance impossible. . . . I also think we can suggest to donors that we want a change in the form in which aid comes. For example, donors no longer should give direct monetary aid, because this can be misutilized, but could provide assistance in other ways that would ensure it is effectively utilized."

Although the discussions on corruption revolved primarily around the return of stolen money, there was general agreement that it will be difficult to achieve democracy without eradicating corruption and establishing effective measures to ensure some level of accountability and transparency in African countries.

FREEDOM OF INFORMATION AND HUMAN RIGHTS

The protection of freedom of information and human rights was identified as a means of bringing about improved governance. One person observed: "The media play a critical role in the maintenance of democracy by providing a bridge between all of the different elements in society." Participants noted how in Africa the media is "often overlooked, yet could provide links among African countries, which at present are too isolated from one another." It was noted that there are nonetheless severe obstacles to their performance of this role. For example, it was stated that almost everywhere in Africa "radio and television are under direct government control. Radio is often particularly important in rural areas, and among people not literate in European languages, whereas newspapers are expensive to run and can be subject to government censorship or indirect pressures over matters such as the supply of newsprint. In countries like Mozambique, the media were assigned a political role as agents of mobilization. In South Africa, although restrictions have been eased, newspapers still retain a high degree of self-censorship."

Participants strongly believed that the media should be free from state control and entrusted to professional journalists who, in areas such as Nigeria and southern Africa, have maintained a courageous commitment to press freedom. It was acknowledged, however, that professional training is needed for journalists, especially in countries whose press has been under state control. One participant called for African journalists to train younger colleagues, organize themselves into associations and trade unions, and to sponsor conferences around the issue of the press and democracy. These steps, he offered, "could contribute to the emergence of a free and independent press in Africa, with persistent reporting in turn contributing to improved governance." Another specific suggestion was for journalists to "move away from lavishly reporting the activities of heads of state to eliciting the help of civic associations in gaining access to alternative news sources, especially in order to penetrate rural areas."

While supporting privatization of the media, participants recognized a danger that, in places such as South Africa, this might concentrate ownership in the hands of the wealthy: "A dispersed and variegated press is needed, including a local press, so that readers can vote with their money against inadequate reporting." A number of participants recommended that, in the interim, state-controlled media should provide equal opportunities of access. It also was pointed out that reforms of press laws will be required in a number of countries. Some participants advocated that a code of ethics for the press be instituted simultaneously with such new laws.

As one participant illustrated, "ultimately, freedom of the press reflects the freedom of society itself. In countries such as Swaziland and Zambia, the refusal of the press to be coopted was a major factor contributing to an open society." Another participant expressed this notion somewhat differently, "I am amazed that the example of the lively free press in Nigeria hasn't been duplicated elsewhere in Africa. In Nigeria, there are over 50 newspapers and lots of magazines, with many of them in local languages and dialects. Generally, the more press there is, the greater the difficulty government has in suppressing it." Freedom of the press is a central area in the whole field of human rights that, participants maintained, needs constant monitoring. Participants indicated that regular indigenous institutions for monitoring should be established, although assistance from international civil society also could be very supportive, ideas that will be discussed further in the next chapter. The use of alternative media, such as drama, news murals, and posters to educate people about rights was also recommended.

DECENTRALIZATION AND DEVOLUTION OF POWER

Political autonomy and policy participation for local communities and ethnic groups in society are significant factors of government legitimacy. Participants noted that, in politically fragmented countries, decentralization might allow the various political, religious, ethnic, or tribal groups greater representation in development decision making, thereby increasing their stake in maintaining political stability. One participant convincingly argued, "With reference to decentralization, I would simply like to say that we have to look at things from the point of view of democratic society. . . . Are we going to tolerate diversity? . . . If it's a dialogue among peers, then we can't concentrate the political and economic power in the hands of just a few people. . . . I think we have to tolerate this diversity, and political and economic decentralization should be admitted as having the right to exist. . . . We do not have to try to achieve uniformity because it is perhaps not the best thing. I think that decentralization of power is not bad. . . . It will, of course mean that there is a limitation on the centralization of power in both the political and economic fields."

There was clear agreement that centralization and personalization of power by rulers has been a major obstacle to democracy in African countries: "Africa's problem is unequivocally and fundamentally political. . . . Political centralization has led to economic centralization, which has led to economic crisis. . . . Institutionally, because most African countries are overly centralized, there needs to be both horizontal and vertical decentralization of power."

One specific suggestion was to decentralize politics first so that the legislative and judicial branches of power could become independent and their powers strengthened, in order to act as a check on the powers of the executive. Participants further pointed out that the power and authority of most African heads of state blatantly override the powers of the legislature and the judiciary. In other words, because of the personalization of power by the rulers, an enormous gap exists between the rulers and the people. In some African countries, constitutions and other laws have been revised to give rulers the right to exercise exceptional powers. For example, in Sierra Leone and Kenya, constitutional amendments and statutory provisions have allowed the presidents to exercise emergency powers anywhere in the country at any time. Most participants believed that, in the future, it would be necessary to limit the excessive concentration of power in the hands of the executive in order to ensure some level of accountability through the other branches of government.

There was a clear sense that the role of the centralized state must be limited. As one person suggested: "Local government must be allowed to work. . . . The state's monopoly control must be broken down. . . . The formal structures in the state are highly centralized, whatever way you look at it. This is the problem as far as the issue of centralization is concerned." Another suggestion was for a reexamination of state-societal relations in the context of decentralization as it relates to democratization. One participant advocated that the state communicate with societal elements, such as clans and tribes, and not just with one ethnic group in society: "Decentralization can absorb ethnic issues at the middle level; groups have something they can control at their level. . . . Decentralization will be territorial and ethnic based." "But minorities will have to be protected, if they live, for example, in the 'wrong' area," argued one participant. Another participant, however, cautioned that decentralization should not be allowed to result in the replacement of authentic, grass roots leaders with party members. In short, the participants agreed that decentralization could be useful in encouraging local autonomy, strengthening civil society at the grass roots level in both rural and urban areas, and providing ways for women to participate in issues of immediate local concern to them.

The discussions on decentralization also focused on the devolution of power. One participant argued that "decentralization has been cloaked in rhetoric without devolution, resulting in the further illegitimacy of the state and the weakness of civil society. As African states became increasingly incapable of delivering [on their economic and political promises], associational life emerged at the local level. This often took the form of a shadow state, where people organized themselves to provide basic services that, in their communities, had been ignored by the state. In this bubbling up process, these groups would then try to extract necessities from the state in order to provide services. Civil society, therefore, emerges in this form to meet basic human needs at the local level, not resulting from macro-level concerns. If there is to be an efficient link between state and society, with effective articulation by associations, then local government, in the form of devolution, would be most appropriate. In this way, devolution could provide the missing link between the center and periphery in rural areas. Yet autonomous local governments hold out important prospects, not only in rural areas, but also in urbanized areas, such as those in South Africa."

Some participants, however, expressed caveats in the discussions about decentralization: "As far as decentralization is concerned, it can be a little dangerous, because the more we try to decentralize, the more we come up against certain community realities that may dismantle or destroy the greater community. . . . In such situations, there is an inordinate amount of stress on certain ethnic communities or characteristics. This may not always be optimal, as far as the Africa of tomorrow is concerned. . . . But, if we are aware of these dangers, I think we can overcome them."

Another participant suggested that societies with diverse ethnic groups centralize power primarily because that has been the easy and cheapest way out of anticipated problems. He maintained, "When we talk of decentralization, I can tell you that I participated in a number of discussions in my country in which the people of certain regions said they were opposed to decentralization because they were the rich sections of the community and they had the mineral resources. Therefore, they argued, they should have more money and their incomes should be bigger than the other areas, as they supply the resources. Consequently, if centralization were developed in some areas, it was because it was the cheapest way out. . . . Democracy, of course, calls for money and for financing."

MODES OF REPRESENTATION

The issue of modes of representation in African countries also was a topic of discussion in the three workshops. Many participants argued that federalism might be the best known mechanism, although not the only method, of giving autonomy to different societal groups, thereby accommodating what participants termed the "ethnic variable." There was some support for regionalism, in the form of a unitary state with some federal character. Yet the difficulty in coming to any clear agreement concerning representation was illustrated by one participant, who asked, "On what does one base federalism? If one resorts to ethnic groups, which primarily are territorially based, then people worry about ethnicity. They see that disputes can lead to intergroup conflicts when groups live in proximity, such as is the case in Lebanon. If groups live in the periphery, it can lead to separatism. . . . If groups are interspersed, then violent conflict can emerge, as it has in the Balkans and in Nagorno-Karabakh. There are no simple solutions."

Another participant further argued, "Regarding the devolution of authority in the form of a federal or regional state, I see a problem with the concept of a federal state dividing the country into local governments that have absolute sovereignty over their units. Can a country, like Ethiopia, staff about 15 different governments? Moreover, I fear that tribal and ethnic problems could emerge, perhaps leading to disintegration, as in Yugoslavia. Therefore, maybe a regional state organized along economic units might make more sense."

Another participant from South Africa expressed similar cynicism: "In talking about regionalism and federalism, is one trying to weaken the central government in order to recognize ethnicity, or in order to ensure that a future, majority-controlled government won't be able to function?" Yet another participant who is engaged in the negotiation process of the Convention for a Democratic South Africa expressed further reservations with the "federal option as it is being used by white South Africans to divide and concentrate power without question. For us, the redistribution of power and resources is essential. Blacks have had to stand up as South Africans who have been victims of apartheid. Is it necessary to recognize ethnicity in order to move to democracy, as in Ethiopia, or should we not keep our South African unity? Whereas the South African government is pushing for the constitutional entrenchment of ethnicity, the African National Congress believes that to be the Soviet model, which it cannot accept. I agree that regional concerns should exist, as should regional governments, but the state should be given central powers to allow it to function effectively and to redistribute resources where needed. To this end, I doubt that the efforts under way in Nigeria would be an option for South Africa."

The question of what kind of future constituencies might be more productive for African countries produced various reactions from participants. Some argued that smaller units might be more manageable, as more people would be involved and ethnic divisions would be minimized, because, in the latter case, the larger ethnic groups would be broken down into smaller states. Others argued that regional representation with bigger followings offers enormous possibilities to help smaller states.

A few participants, however, advocated representation based on something more than territorial constituencies. This view was well argued by one participant: "Initially, representation was territorially based, which is the basic system almost everywhere. But, in Eastern Europe, as in Africa, it has been argued that territorial representation isn't enough. One also needs functional representation, perhaps through an electoral college, where individuals would represent functional groups. In the French Fourth Republic, for example, this took the form of an economic and social council." Another participant pointed out that Namibia was undertaking to "capture with representation the influence of traditional rulers in rural areas," by incorporating functional representation into government through the establishment of a second House. The crucial point to be made is that, democracy must always be prepared to recognize differences among groups of people, but whether these should be institutionalized within a federal system is something that may legitimately vary from state to state. A nonfederal Nigeria, for example, is barely conceivable, but federal systems in other states may carry different implications. If federalism is to work, there must be a real commitment to the center, as well as to the individual units. As the former

Soviet Union and Yugoslavia demonstrate, federalism does not provide a means of keeping together peoples who don't want to stay together anyhow.

Despite the overwhelming acknowledgment that effective systems of governance are needed in African countries, participants were unsure of how African countries could proceed to create new models of governance in a climate of decline and economic stagnation. To this end, there was a strong sense among participants that donors need to address the linkages between the economic and political reforms they suggest to African countries, particularly in relation to their compatibility and sequencing. Participants noted how economic reforms have caused deep despair, unemployment, and malnutrition and have not been as successful as was originally hoped. In this context, it also was noted that many African governments have become more, not less, authoritarian since they accepted such conditionalities on economic assistance. The government of Ghana, for example, "was able to carry out its reforms because it used force." In the future, participants thought that, before imposing conditions, donors should encourage discussions and seek consensus through dialogue with African countries.

4

Institutions Needed to Sustain Democracy

Institutional weakness has been widely documented by scholars and policy makers as a notable problem in Sub-Saharan Africa. The weakness of African institutions has become a significant issue primarily because the difficulty of realizing the benefits of development programs and projects, especially those funded by bilateral and multilateral donors, has been blamed on underdeveloped and inefficient institutions in most African countries. In order for African countries to succeed in the development process, appropriate institutions based on democratic values need to be established in their countries that will contribute to development and improved governance.

In addition to a country's constitution and its critical provisions—freedom of expression, freedom of association, and rule of law—governance-related institutions such as the civil service, the judiciary, and other local institutions need to be developed in African countries to play a role in the development and maintenance of a democratic culture. Developing and sustaining democratic institutions in African countries with the assistance of donors should receive special attention, since the inability of these institutions to implement policies to ensure development has been an impediment to democracy. For example, donor countries maintain that political stagnation, repression, and corruption in Africa now constitute the greatest obstacles to badly needed outside investment and significant economic growth.

The workshop discussions that concerned sustaining democracy through institutional measures were grounded on the common belief that the process of building democracy is never complete. In likening democracy to an "ongoing experiment that never finishes," participants indicated that democracy is both a process and a goal. They pointed out that where democratic ventures have been successful, there has been continuous consultation, multiple points of access to decision making, and the empowerment of individuals to participate. "This is why the democratic experiment remains an experiment and why the structures put in place can continue to be reshaped as time goes on."

Botswana was cited as an example of an African country that has transparency not only in decision making but also because it offers an example of "input that continually recharges the batteries" of government, and that the "doors of government are open." One participant commented: "One can voice a complaint and get things done—and not just through one's representative in the national assembly. . . . Because party politics in Botswana are partially separated from the administration of the country, one can get a complaint processed through one's party representative, local chief, or local councils, because the government listens [to these actors]." Thus, the significant point to note here is that the existence of plural institutions within government guarantees to various groups alternative mechanisms by which they can get a response from government. It was also pointed out that the more individuals participate in building a democratic society, the less power particular groups, such as ethnic groups, economic interest groups, and, perhaps, even the military, are able to exercise: "Empowerment to participate may have its dangers, but it certainly can mitigate the strengths of veto groups in society."

Participants indicated that retaining the possibility of change may be the greatest secret of success in democracies. They made the point that the multiple possibilities for redress and change in democratic systems is what drives citizens to participate. As one put it, "In the case of Botswana, what has kept the system going is that elections have been relatively honest; the government has, in fact, kept its promises by and large, and has remained popular; and the opposition continues to act as a loyal opposition, believing sincerely in the possibility of alternation." There was general agreement that, if there is a formula, it is to maintain the possibility of change: "By keeping open the various doors to political innovation, it becomes possible to change policies, to continue the experiment under different auspices." In sum, participants underscored that the possibility of change in a system, honestly believed by its citizens, is a key factor in sustaining functioning democracies.

Effective institutions to sustain democracy are needed in Africa given the failure of formally organized structures, most of which were inherited from the colonial period. The workshop participants discussed political and other institutions that in most cases symbolize a commitment to democracy, such as separation of powers, an independent press, electoral systems, civil service—institutions that have not been effective in African countries. But the central focus of the discussions on sustaining democracy centered on constitutions, the military, independent commissions, and a transnational democratic center. These were believed to be the key institutions that can significantly contribute to sustaining democracy if they become effective in their roles. Participants chose not to spend time discussing the traditional institutions in detail, electing instead to address the problems that prevent such institutions from performing effectively.

CONSTITUTIONS

A significant development in the three workshops was the renewed advocacy of constitutionalism in Africa. African regimes, under domestic or external pressures from donor countries, and perhaps to reinstall their credibility with the Western world, are experimenting with their constitutions on the path of political liberalization as seen in recent constitutional amendments in countries such as Sierra Leone, Ghana, Algeria, and Uganda. Africans are now challenging the deep-rooted primacy of the African chief by consulting constitutions and inserting new devices in them with the intention of decentralizing power.

There was clear agreement among participants that, if the central problem of democracy is the relationship between the individual and the state, then the quest for limited government, embodied in constitutionalism, is a feature of every society and not just a Western concept. Just as many precolonial African societies shared unwritten rules regarding tyranny, a practice of limited government could be identified in few postindependence African countries, although it failed in many. Participants devoted much discussion to why constitutionalism had failed. They were careful, however, to frame the discussion from the perspective that "Africa was ushering in a period of liberalism and democracy after 30 years of authoritarianism in most countries, whereas it took Europe 300 years to consolidate that process."

In general, colonialism was said to have been a poor school of constitutionalism. The colonists had offered Africans the opportunity to organize and practice limited government only in the terminal years of their rule, but, in a number of countries where liberation was achieved through armed struggle, this opportunity was not offered. It was pointed out that "one doesn't learn democracy in haste, but over time, through trust in others, linkages, and coalition building." Participants noted that constitutions had been developed in great haste, some of which proved totally unworkable. For example, in several countries, the constitutional protections for minority groups and whites ran against majority preferences, leading to subsequent efforts by majority coalitions to overturn the constitution, as is currently the case in South Africa. Several participants recalled the history of moves to de facto single-party rule in their countries. One participant noted that the "alien character of new constitutions posed problems of acceptability, which were compounded by unpropitious conditions and the inheritance of the colonial state." As the constitution became the center of controversy in African states, "it was not long before the freedoms and rights in the constitution were eroded by the state."

A participant with legal experience observed that constitutions in the postcolonial period "have been in the desk drawers, having been honored more in breach than in observance," and cited a number of the commonly circulated justifications for the failure of constitutionalism in Africa. "The notion that, in the past, decisions were arrived at by consensus; the fact that African leaders were chosen by heredity or emerged through proven leadership, were obeyed, and were rarely removed; the idea that individuals are more concerned with their daily bread than with constitutional rights; that issues of hunger, famine, health, roads, etc., were the real priorities—these arguments do not tell the whole story and are sad echoes of the ideas advanced by the colonists at the end of the colonial period." Then turning to the notion that "constitutions are inspired by imported, alien Western principles," the same participant noted a double standard to the argument, pointing out that "the arguments made by Africans rejecting constitutionalism were similar to the arguments they advanced justifying the adoption of [Soviet-style] authoritarianism."

Yet another participant illustrated the failure of constitutionalism somewhat differently. Africans, he said, had created incentives for excesses and abuses by those in power, and they occurred. "Our own impatience," he then offered, "had led us to think the constitution had failed, even if a particular crisis is supposed to be part of a learning process. African militaries are guilty of making this judgment." In Nigeria, for example, manipulation of the ballot box was said to have provided the excuse for military intervention in order to "save" the constitution, which actually resulted in its suspension. Moreover, the lack of congruence between written and unwritten constitutions in Africa, between formal rules and unwritten norms, in his opinion, also had contributed to the demise of constitutionalism.

There was agreement among participants that at the close of the colonial period, the newly written constitutions had not been rooted in the societies in which they were to operate. By advocating an examination of the colonial constitutions, participants believed they might shed some light on why limited government survived or did not. It was further suggested that one relate constitutions to their contexts in order to avoid another backslide to authoritarianism. In this current effort, "democracy must take into account the realities of the people, their political experience, and their history." Yet several participants cautioned that "African heritage would not be too useful in the sociopolitical point of view with regard to formal institutions in the political field, such as the separation of powers."

The starting point of rooting and anchoring constitutions in Africa, suggested another participant, "would be to go back to the people, who must decide, define, and approve their system of government. Such a process has a chance of resulting in individuals with an interest in safeguarding their constitution, because they will demand the rights due to them as inalienable and their birthright." Other participants concurred on the need to bridge the gap between the ideal and reality by "incorporating the values a political community holds dear," because "African history reveals that the problem is how to bring theoretical norms into practice. In the past, our liberal constitutions were not respected or practiced." It was also pointed out that because constitutions are intended to derive their whole authority from the governed, ratification would be essential in this second round of African liberation: "Power must originate from and then evolve with the participation of the majority of the people."

There was general agreement that, if democracy is to be sustained in Africa, new constitutions should be written, setting down a covenant between state and society in which political and other state powers are bound by rules. It was suggested that new constitutions should constitute "the organic or fundamental law of the state, establishing the character and conceptions of its government, organizing the government and regulating, distributing, and limiting the functions of its different departments, as well as prescribing the extent and manner of the exercise of its sovereign powers." By adopting new rules of the game, it was suggested that the legacy of arbitrariness might be curbed, while giving room for civil liberties. In this manner, "democracy will serve as a contract between the rulers and the ruled for a period—for some people, four years; for others, five years. Then one renews the contract. We have the power; the power belongs to the people. Within this period, government will give us the opportunity to exercise that power, that sacred trust of surrendering one's power to rule oneself, to this body of people, for that period of time, for definite purposes, such as to protect one's life. These are the conditions in which, by organizing the state, one is allowed the freedoms of association, assembly, religion, economy, and so on."

In the Namibia workshop, a minimum of guarantees was identified to ensure that democracy would be upheld by the constitution. They included a bill of rights, limited tenure in government office, regular elections and the power of impeachment, protection for various groups (including ethnic groups, parties, unions, etc.), checks and balances, an independent judiciary and legislature, and an amendment process. The latter was of particular significance, in the view of several participants, because the "constitution should be seen as a document outlining the rules and/or guidelines of a process and not be static."

Although participants in the three workshops were hesitant to spell out the contents of a typical bill of rights, they did underline that new constitutions must enshrine human rights and "not only be based on the rule of law." One telling example in support of this principle was the case of a citizen who had written a letter to the editor of his local paper in which he accused the president of bankrupting the country, economically and politically. Through a manipulative penal code and legal system, the state was able to jail the individual for the basic expression of political belief, try him as a common criminal, and pronounce sentence, although public outrage resulted in the latter's suspension.

One view was that it would be more appropriate for "government to enforce rights and obligations by allowing an effective and freely elected parliament, with the recognition of the value of an opposition, as well as to facilitate academic freedom in the universities." On one hand, several participants advanced the idea that, in order to enable citizens to work nonviolently against the emergence of future dictatorships, the rights to dissent, to demonstrate in public, and to stage popular uprisings should be enshrined in the constitution. On the other hand, although specific checks and balances were not endorsed, many suggestions were floated, including a bicameral legislature, budget and control over the military assigned to the legislature, and a presidential veto.

In the Benin workshop, one participant pointed out that a great challenge for constitution writers and founders today in Africa is to make decisions about elections and representation. He advocated a careful examination of the "different devices of elections—such as proportional representation, single-member districts, electoral colleges, proportional representation with preferential voting, and primaries—the sorts of devices that have been used in the past in other societies, as well as the relationship between those devices and the establishment of democracy in a fashion that is more likely to be sustained than if other systems are used."

The participants in the Namibia workshop were of the opinion that the implementation of constitutional provisions would require demystification of the constitution through its wide dissemination and through civic education; a neutral, highly motivated, and effectively decentralized civil service; a strengthened legislature with its own trained staff, institutional memory, and adequate facilities; an independent judiciary; a free press; and a reconstituted military, which is discussed below. Participants suggested that the legislative and judicial branches of government could be strengthened by the presence of a strong civil society and an independent watchdog press, strong subnational institutions at the state and local level, adequate pay, and a code of conduct.

Although the discussions on separation of powers were brief in all three workshops, there was a clear understanding that the branches of government must have the means to carry out their tasks competently. In newly democratic countries, it was noted, "the legislature often has no power and is not respected. It cannot even adopt its own budget, because the state itself is of the opinion that the resources are not available for this. Without financial autonomy, can there be a state of law? Can the legislature play the role it was assigned?" An additional measure to enable the legislature to serve as an alternative center of power to the executive, participants suggested, would be the empowerment of opposition political parties. One participant, however, cautioned that there must be a concomitant democratization of political parties.

In order to ensure the independence of the judiciary, participants indicated that independent commissions could be established to appoint judges in each African country. As there was much concern voiced about whether the judicial system would be able to reach the rural areas, one participant suggested that judges could be required to go on circuit. Another suggestion was that perhaps practitioners of customary law could be incorporated into the judicial system at the grass roots level.

In general, there was a sense among participants that the branches of government, "whether we are talking about the legislature, the judiciary, or the executive, are institutions with new roles to play. They have to know the rules of the game and stick to them. It will be incumbent upon them to act in conformity with the stipulations of the constitution." It was the opinion of many participants that African states would not overnight become democratic; they will make mistakes. Yet the hope was that institutionalizing democratic norms in the constitution would go a long way toward sowing democratic culture within African societies.

RECONSTITUTING THE MILITARY

In the three workshops, there was clear agreement that, if the constitution is not to live under constant threat, the capacity of the military to seize power at will had to be removed. Participants displayed a remarkable determination to examine and confront the role of force in African politics. "We are at a stage in Africa where, for the most part, one should concentrate on those social and political forces, such as the potential for military coups d'état, that may possibly endanger the early sustenance of democracy."

As the discussion focused on the need to provide incentives for some form of disarmament and reduction of the sheer size of the military in African society, participants were quick to identify the central dilemma: How to persuade present-day militaries that reductions are in their interest.

Participants assumed, for purposes of the discussion, that the military would be placed under effective civilian control following the transition, and the policy problem would be how to keep them there. From this point onward, opinion was divided, with most participants arguing that the military should be kept out of politics and redirected into productive sectors of the economy, while a small yet significant number advocated that the military establishment should not be kept outside the transition process to democracy. In addition, participants in each of the workshops questioned the necessity to maintain militaries in Africa, particularly in light of the large share of national resources they consume.

In discussing strategies to contain the military and reduce the burden they impose on fragile economies, several participants pointed out that, historically, efforts to reduce military spending or numbers of troops have served "as the very reason why it [the military] has interfered in political life." One illustration was that because the military in Sierra Leone enjoys special privileges, such as buying goods at heavily subsidized prices, they would be likely to resist strongly if the economy is liberalized and their budget is slashed. For these reasons, participants in the Namibia workshop advocated confronting the military with great caution and in a gradual manner. They identified as an obvious first start having civilians define precisely the functions of the country's security forces, while phasing out paramilitary forces. Another measure would be to reduce the military's size through attrition and by suspending recruitment. They underscored that these measures should be undertaken concurrently with providing civic education to the military. Put somewhat differently by one participant in the Ethiopia workshop, it would be necessary to "demystify the gun" in African society, which could be accomplished "by educating civilians about the nature and function of the army." In contrast, a more radical approach was suggested by at least one participant in Ethiopia: "The first step toward demilitarization should be a reduction in the military budget."

In the three meetings, participants held the view that African militaries would do well to become professional and disciplined, conscious of human rights standards and protections, and productive. Several participants recalled how a number of standing militaries had asked for seminars on democracy, which, they suggested, should be organized without delay, and that help in educating and professionalizing the military should be part of the assistance strategies employed by donor countries.

Although the current Nigerian case of military cooperation with the transition to democracy was cited, most participants remained skeptical about the military role in politics. One person recommended that "when soldiers want to become politicians, they can't be part of the armed forces, and, if they want to go back to military service, they can't be politicians." Out of a profound distrust of the military, most participants advocated transforming

African militaries into technicians. In Guinea, plans are under way to assign the military to work in many different fields, including road maintenance and farming, so that they would not be idle. In Niger, because the military possesses the necessary human and material resources, it is likely to be building roads through currently impassable areas, constructing schools, and assisting with other productive activities that benefit the society as a whole. Another participant reminded the group in Benin that "the Egyptian army, with all its shortcomings, has one of the best contracting engineering corps, which makes not only roads in Egypt, but bids for contracts elsewhere, producing some of the finest roads and houses around. At the same time, the Egyptian army has one of the best dairy industries in Africa." Others disagreed strongly, cautioning against reinforcing the military's sense that it is the only competent institution in society by assigning it key development roles. Nevertheless, for some participants, the underlying idea remained: the military could contribute to development if it were reconverted, but ought not be integrated into the democratic process.

A distinctly opposite approach—making the military part and parcel of a democratic government—found some limited support at the three meetings. A few participants argued that institutionalizing African militaries so they would not feel alienated would make it unlikely that they would act against the democratic process. One participant advocated institutionalizing the participation of the military in some form, thereby giving them a stake in the democratic process. He recalled a former practice in Great Britain, whereby those at Cambridge and Oxford universities could vote twice in the country's elections. "If academics, then why not soldiers? . . . Although this is a bitter pill, it is a way for fragile, new democracies to associate the military with the fruits of power." Expressed somewhat differently, a number of participants indicated that the military could be fully politicized as a vanguard for democracy, but there were no practical suggestions on how this might be accomplished.

A number of participants expressed profound disagreement with the notion of incorporating the military in the democratic process. One commented: "It seems to me it would be like regularly offering a bribe to a robber so he doesn't rob your house. Both as a matter of principle and empirically, if we look at societies that have given the military a special position, the problems of military interference have not been avoided. An example of this was in Brazil before Collor's election as president, where the military has given up power with the provision that everyone in the political system there accepts that the military can continue to have a kind of veto over all decisions. I'm not sure what you gain in the long run, other than getting the robber to expect a bribe." For most participants, the particularly worrisome element posed by this integration of the military is its reserved right to intervene when certain principles are violated in some fashion. The vague and open nature of the military veto, feared a number of participants, could result in the military's involvement remaining a permanent feature of African politics, rather than a temporary measure of enticement.

In the Namibia meeting, after a particularly intense and thought-provoking small working group, a concrete suggestion was proposed to the plenary session—that "a phased reduction of the military should be undertaken, tied to a fixed-level percentage of the gross domestic product, with a phased redeployment for national service, such as public works projects." This sentiment, although expressed somewhat differently, was offered by a participant in the earlier workshop in Ethiopia, who asked, "Could we not also aim to limit the armed forces in the constitution, with any necessary expansion being subject to a popular referendum?"

A few other novel suggestions included creating an African high command to counter military excesses as they occur in individual countries and revisiting the concept that only presidents appoint personnel to important military posts.

In the three workshops, participants noted that donor assistance would facilitate the restructuring of African militaries. "Donors bear a responsibility in phasing out military assistance and equipment, while supporting the redeployment and retraining of domestic militaries, because they were involved in the military build-up of Africa." The difficulty of achieving the goal of reduced military presence was, however, illustrated by the decision of the Namibian government taken during the time of the workshop in Windhoek to increase the size of the Namibian army in order to provide employment to young South West African People's Organization (SWAPO) loyalists facing widespread unemployment.

INDEPENDENT COMMISSIONS

In the three meetings, a recurring theme was that civil society was closely linked to the institutionalization of democracy. According to a number of academicians, if institutions and leadership could be developed within civil society, creating the conditions for a reemergence of trust between government and the governed, "that would go a long way toward sustaining democracy."

Much attention focused on the role of national commissions on democracy and human rights, which have been established in a number of African states. Participants noted that these institutions have begun to play an important role in monitoring human rights violations, particularly in light of their links to international human rights organizations. Participants stressed that such leagues also represent an attempt to institutionalize democracy in given countries.

In Nigeria, for example, it was pointed out that the Center for Democratic Studies has been operating since 1987, conducting research on democracy out of the belief that "it should not be assumed that people know what democracy is. Even the legislators should be taught tolerance, to give and take, and that it is not a crime to be in the opposition." Several Nigerian participants advocated that similar "centers for research in political science or the social sciences be created across the continent, so that certain democratic processes can be anticipated on the basis of research carried out." Another participant cited how, in Niger, a number of commissions had been set up to "control the activities of government," including the High Council for Communication, which "enables the leaders of various groups in the country to express themselves freely on the radio and in the press, to denounce abuses, and to engage in democratic discussions." One participant from Benin, however, in noting the plethora of new institutions in his country, lamented that they "have been dragging their feet lately."

One noteworthy discussion centered on what it is about independent commissions that has made them relatively successful. One participant summarized: "First, what independent institutions, associations, and projects have in common is that they all involve people in a common effort. . . . The success of some of these institutions is due to their increasing the range of participation, that is, giving people access to share their views and concerns, and letting them become partners in the enterprise."

A number of participants in the Benin workshop expressed concern about the objectivity of institutions in Africa. Nevertheless, others felt that individuals could press their governments to allow independent institutions to emerge by carefully examining the international treaty obligations undertaken by their particular countries. One commented: "Under international law, the UN human rights covenants, and the African Charter on Human and Peoples Rights, African governments are obliged to create institutions that are dedicated to the promotion of democratic principles and human rights, to encourage those that already have been established, and [to enable] the separation of powers and the building of a strong and independent judiciary." Individuals, he argued, would have to urge their governments to "pay more than lip service to the obligations they have undertaken" and could seek the assistance of donor countries in the process.

Other participants advocated that independent commissions be built into new African constitutions: "National commissions for democracy and human rights could be established in each country, with their status, power, and functions spelled out in the constitution so that government does not bend the constitution to suit its interests. . . . Such commissions, funded and operated independent of the government, might help build the necessary confidence for civil society to emerge."

In Ethiopia, one participant indicated that, once national institutions were established, "general guidelines could be made known, which would then allow for all sorts of associations at the grass roots level to become useful organs for a new political culture in Africa." To this end, another participant in the Ethiopia meeting believed that a consensus document "setting out what constitutes civil society and what democracy is should be decided at the national level and then distributed." Nevertheless, the general sentiment seemed headed in the other direction, favoring autonomous decision making within independent commissions.

In the three workshops, independent electoral commissions were identified as critical to sustaining democracy. Most participants agreed that such commissions should not be appointed by government, as it would have to act as referee at the time of elections. Yet, in the Benin workshop, one participant argued that effective work can be carried out, despite an initial government role: "My organization was established with loyalty to the center. All members are appointed centrally. We are tasked with raising the political consciousness of the people toward the state or the nation, rather than toward its constituent parts. . . . Essentially, we are organizing national, state, and local elections, dividing the country into senatorial districts and federal constituencies and articulating the guidelines for the establishment of political parties."

There was a clear understanding that the role of independent electoral commissions would be to register voters, organize and supervise elections, and monitor and evaluate electoral results. One participant commented: "Things have to be quite clear as far as ensuring a proper situation during a vote. The last time we had elections, there were no identity cards and no monitoring body. The next time, we can't do that. The Ministry of the Interior should no longer be solely responsible for physically carrying the ballot boxes and ballots. There has to be somebody else responsible, some monitoring agency, which would contribute to the truthfulness of the results of the ballot." One specific recommendation was that electoral commissions have consolidated revenue funds, which would be independent of the government administration.

There was no clear agreement, however, on whether international observers should necessarily be a part of this process. Most participants agreed that international observers would be useful during one or two national elections subsequent to a country's undergoing or having completed a transition to democracy. And yet one participant in Ethiopia pointed out, "Although international observers are important during a transitional period, as they serve to help fledgling democracies, one might not want to be judged to be a complete failure for having failed once. In other words, a permanent provision for outside monitors cannot be accepted by countries whose citizenry feels confident with their electoral system." Still, it was clear that independent electoral commissions could help ensure participation in the voting process by seeing that future elections in Africa would be conducted in a free and fair manner.

TRANSNATIONAL DEMOCRATIC CENTER

In the three meetings, there was widespread agreement that an Africa-wide reinforcement of democratization is needed. One person remarked: "I think that, up to now, we haven't referred to an inter-African dimension, which is very important as far as democracy is concerned. This is a dimension that we must not forget. That is, we ought to go beyond the state as it now exists to create certain trans-state structures, African in nature." Participants suggested that there ought to be a transnational network to serve as a support system for democracy, so that if there is trouble in one country, a group from another country could come to its assistance. The idea was that the transnational center could launch pleas for urgent action, thereby setting in motion the intervention of watchdog organizations concerned when rights are threatened.

By facilitating the emergence of a pan-African network, participants noted that a transnational center also might serve to make domestic groups more professional. In Namibia participants further elaborated that the transnational center would draw on African resources in support of democracy, conduct research and training activities, and assist with information sharing in two-way exchanges.

There was agreement across the three workshops that, by linking up, Africans would rely on themselves and not the West, thereby lessening the "stigma of Europeans being brought in." Nevertheless, participants recognized that limited resources might impede the ability of such a center to actually perform the tasks envisioned. It was noted that "it will be difficult for groups to create a permanent network because they lack material and there is a difficulty of movement and the free flow of information among countries." For these reasons, some participants advocated starting up regional democratic centers as a first step. Others thought that computers, modems, and electronic mail, which are appearing increasingly throughout Africa, could provide a sufficient level of infrastructure to facilitate communication among the constituent groups of the future transnational center. A number of participants in the Ethiopia workshop advocated seeking external assistance for a transnational center, declaring it "imperative that domestic organizations be helped materially and be assisted in creating a network at the pan-African level."

Still other participants cautioned that there is no particular formula to guarantee that domestic human rights and prodemocracy groups will emerge and necessarily hook up with a transnational center. Yet, there was a clear sense among participants that in order to catalyze collective action, individuals and domestic groups must begin to encourage people to protect each other. As one participant pointed out, "One is one's best protector if individuals act collectively when one of them is threatened." Some participants argued that because domestic groups have been atomized, an umbrella organization would be useful, helping to coordinate civil society's autonomous groups, offering guidelines, and, when need be, exposing problems continentwide. The point was also made by some that, "if one builds an umbrella, it might be more easily torn down by the state." To that end, they indicated that informal coalitions might be more useful. Nevertheless, there was strong agreement that a forum within the Organization of African Unity was not what participants had in mind for a transnational democratic center. "The OAU has a tendency to be fuzzy. To encourage people, we must form domestic human rights organizations and then a transnational one, which will build a network among the emerging groups, similar to the Helsinki process."

The strength of this idea was demonstrated by participants in the Namibia meeting, who labored well into the final night of the gathering in order to draft a charter establishing the first transnational democratic center in Africa. With a provisional secretariat in Lesotho, the group aims to build the pan-African network initially among the participants of the three workshops, with ambitious plans to expand to a presence in every African country.

Underlying the above discussions concerning the institutions necessary to sustain democracy was the recognition that democracy can be a costly form of government. Accordingly, one readily identifiable fear among participants in the three workshops was that Africa's unfavorable economic conditions might limit opportunities for sustaining democracy. One participant asked, "Can one be sure in newly democratic states that the citizenry will continue to support a civilian government undertaking painful reforms without external economic assistance?" In this context, participants advocated donor assistance in developing techniques not only to manage the work of democracy, but also to transcend poverty. Some of these issues are discussed in the following chapter.

5

Role of Extra-African Forces in Democratization

Africans have a profound desire for autonomy and independence, but they are recognizing and coming to terms with their incorporation into the international community on a generally dependent basis. In the three meetings, there was clear agreement that Africans must devise democratization programs based on their own indigenous experiences, because without African initiatives no amount of external assistance would bring about democratization on the continent. Participants were of the opinion that the challenge facing Africans today is to manage their relations with the international community in such a way as to promote their own aspirations.

Although participants recognized that the primary burden and future of democracy in Africa is likely to remain on the shoulders of Africans, whether they succeed may depend in part on the international environment in which extra-African forces play a decisive role. These extra-African forces, which will either facilitate or hinder the democratization process under way in Africa, were identified as pro-African lobbies, international financial institutions (notably the World Bank and the International Monetary Fund), regional agencies (such as the United Nations Development Program and its Economic Commission for Africa), private foundations such as Ford or Rockefeller Foundations, as well as multilateral and bilateral donors.

In the past, participants argued, donor involvement in Africa often has been ambivalent or, in some cases, downright harmful. The concentration of assistance in the hands of the few, for example, had enabled some governments to build levels of repressive power that democratic movements now are striving to reduce. Governments that now vehemently complain about external infringements on their sovereignty were once willing to accept aid from donor countries with stringent conditionalities. As a result, participants indicated that the actions of external powers understandably may be viewed with skepticism. They further argued that, although the end of the cold war removed incentives for Western powers to support undemocratic African governments, the absence of cold war competition also significantly reduced African bargaining power and intensified African uneasiness over their dependence on the West.

While the struggle for democratization must always depend primarily on African peoples, there was a clear recognition, nevertheless, that external support has been very important. One participant observed: "Democratization is not possible in Africa without external assistance. . . . I am saying this looking closely at history both within and outside Africa. . . . Virtually no country in the world democratized without some form of foreign assistance. When one looks at countries such as Kenya and Zaire, external assistance has been extremely significant in deciding and, to some extent, helping African leaders accept democratization, which is not an easy option."

In South Africa, for example, moral and subsequently diplomatic and material support for the end of apartheid has helped to sustain the internal liberation movements, with the strong support of other African states proving particularly valuable. External actions, such as the international boycott of sporting events, has helped shake the morale of the white minority community, and external pressure favoring the CODESA effort continues to be helpful. In Madagascar, the campaign in favor of human rights was aided by a speech given by French President François Mitterand while visiting that country. In Zambia, the assistance provided by the Carter Center to monitor the recent presidential elections and to train Zambians to do the same gave legitimacy to what otherwise might have been a questionable operation. In other African countries, the National Democratic Institute of the United States also has conducted training programs in election monitoring.

Several participants, especially in the Benin workshop, advised that a much broader look at the donor-African relationship be taken. Said one participant, "Shakespeare in *The Tempest* says at one point that 'misery acquaints a man with strange bedfellows.'. . . I find it ironic that the prodemocratic forces in Africa are expecting so much from the donors. . . . After all, the progressive forces in Africa historically have been rather antidonor, speaking of neocolonialism and such things. In this time of great need, however, there is a willingness to go to bed with the donors and to expect quite a lot from them. . . . I think that's very dangerous, because (to switch metaphors) one should be very wary of the guest who won't leave at the end of the dinner party. . . . In recent years and more so in some countries than in others, donors have forced political conditionality on recalcitrant regimes. The American embassy, for example, has been a force for democratization in a country like Kenya. . . . I have heard that donors had some influence in the transition process here in Benin, too. But the question is, should donors continue this role once the transition process is finished? If U.S. embassies become accustomed to imposing political conditionality, at what point does that stop? I propose to you that it is an extremely tough question and that the willingness to invite donors into the policy process should be thought out very carefully."

Although various ideas were expressed concerning the proper role of donors before and after the transition to democracy, there was a clear acknowledgment that external actors have their own agendas. Despite few African states having acceptable human rights records, it was argued that external actors selectively intervene in order to support their own interests. One observer remarked: "In view of donors putting democracy on the agenda, Africans are bound to ask why the West and its institutions are insisting on democracy now, when over the years they have provided the means to keep democracy away. Is it because they have changed the rules? If so, how should Africans respond? I would argue that we either adapt or die."

Participants pointed out the central dilemmas Africans face when discussing the role of extra-African forces in the democratization process are determining when assistance turns to dictation and what level of commitment aid donors might be ready to make in order to advance African democratization. In the discussions concerning these questions, participants identified several problems in the pattern of external assistance to Africa.

PROBLEMS WITH AID IN AFRICA

The first problem participants identified concerned the level of aid Africa receives from extra-African forces. Arguing that insufficient aid has been a constant, they noted how a shrinking global economy seems to be preventing donor countries from giving Africa the aid it needs. Participants pointed out how only a minuscule amount of available aid goes to Africa, while allotments to developed countries in Eastern Europe and the former Soviet Union are increasing: "The postcolonial African state has lived off aid and trade. . . . It had prospered from trade, but progressively killed it off, growing increasingly dependent on aid. Today, the average African country derives between 15 and 30 percent of its budget through aid. . . . African countries have accepted this state of affairs because they have no choice. The donors have accepted it because of the cold war and other geostrategic concerns. . . . When the cold war ended, budget difficulties in the domestic economies of the West were increasing. Within donor agencies, too, there has been growing unhappiness with the ineffectiveness of aid."

The second problem participants identified dealt with the types of aid Africa receives—military hardware, capital-intensive projects, salaries to professionals hired by donors, etc.—which they argued are not very useful: "We should differentiate between strategic and tactical aid. . . . Strengthening the economic potential of democratization, akin to a Marshall plan for Africa, is needed in order to create a national alliance. . . . This would enable us to build on surplus in order to allow our patriotic forces to gain ascendance. . . . If such strategic aid is not forthcoming, then tactical aid won't have much impact. . . . Most aid falls into the tactical area, which actually facilitates the drain on resources."

The relationship between donors and recipients was characterized by net capital outflows from Africa. Participants argued there was no point in giving development assistance to corrupt governments that have shown very little desire or ability to use public resources for the public good: "Some donors become corruptors as they collude with corrupt leaders in transactions that are not transparent. . . . Aid is given and siphoned back by corrupt leaders to the giver country," said one participant. It was also suggested that granting new loans to African countries might not necessarily help democratization thrive and could magnify existing problems. Participants argued that, although it would not be easy to grant debt forgiveness, it would be unreasonable for donors to demand that African countries continue to use disproportionate amounts of their resources for debt servicing.

A third area concerned the aid process, which often "impinges on the sovereignty of African nations by dictating, imposing, or otherwise predetermining the content of projects." Structural adjustment, one participant argued, was an example of a policy with limited success, in part because most countries lack the skills necessary to institute adjustment programs. More importantly, it was observed that "the political will is just not there, because one is asking government officials to reduce the opportunities that they have to help their cronies, which raises fundamental problems." Another participant, in concurring with these ideas, held that the "overall relationship between donors and recipient nations tends to be uneven."

CHALLENGES FACED BY AFRICAN COUNTRIES

African countries face a simultaneity of challenges. Most important, participants noted a decline in economic performances. Illustrating Africa's economic decline, one participant pointed out that "the only time African countries experienced economic growth was the period following the attainment of independence. In the face of faltering economies, Africans, like the rest of the world, also are confronting problems of health, AIDS, and the environment—the policy environment—and political problems as well, with little help available. . . . Due to our extreme marginalization in the global economy, prospects for foreign aid are extremely limited, especially when we must compete with the rest of the world, particularly Eastern Europeans, for an ever shrinking pot of money."

Participants suggested that despite the obvious linkages between political and economic reform, one should not be a prerequisite for the other. They also argued that economic reform programs, which predated democratization and governance reforms, generally had not succeeded, in part because they "had no clearly articulated linkages with political reform efforts, even though it was clear that the problems in Africa were political." Some even argued that the emphasis on economic reforms had not been conducive of political reforms. To this end, one African expressed the cynical view of a number of participants that the "economic context of democratic transition is one of stagnation and decline, primarily because the West asks for democratic reciprocal action from African countries in exchange for assistance to them."

Participants further examined the relationship between democracy and economic liberalization, particularly in light of how Africans have little choice or input regarding economic liberalization plans. Structural adjustment reforms, for example, have in most cases produced inflation, unemployment, and frozen wages, in turn resulting in major disturbances. In some countries, the mere acceptance of structural adjustment programs has led to widespread protests and strikes, prompting some governments to use force and coercion in order to proceed with implementation. One participant further argued, "The externals have demonstrated insensitivity to the African political milieu, moving from assistance to dictation, which spells political suicide in Africa. In the future, conditionalities should be country specific." Another participant pondered whether Africa was so poor as to need structural adjustment. Following that line of thinking, yet another thought that Africans would do well in the future "not to implement fully some of the dictates of structural adjustment, calling the bluffs of international financial institutions when need be."

In the three workshops, there was a clear understanding that Africans do accept the reality that donors will continue to press for political and economic reforms as preconditions for aid. Participants were distressed, however, that donors often send mixed signals to African countries, especially regarding the correlation between democracy and reforms. One suggested: "It is important to tell donors, especially the Agency for International Development, that giving contradictory signals is not conducive to democratization or economic development in Africa. . . . The United States of America does not have a history of support for democracy, because it has supported antidemocratic forces in Africa and other areas—Augusto Pinochet and Zia ul-Haq—and continues to be the basis of the survival of Mobutu Sese Seko and Dr. Kamuzu Banda. In the future, donors should listen more to Africans in order to better help us, be sensitive to our situation so they may more effectively come to our aid."

Although questions were raised about the relationship between the sincerity of the donors' promotion of democratization and commitment to further assistance for Africa, several participants thought it would be more beneficial if Africans assume that donors are ready to support democracy in Africa. As one participant noted, "The role and record of the United States, for example, have been mixed and ambiguous. . . . We need to set conditions so both donors and recipients benefit from their relationship. . . . Under what conditions can this new donor orientation be helpful to Africans? What conditions should Africans make?"

ROLE OF DONORS IN DEMOCRATIZATION

Assisting Political Change

In the workshops, discussions concerning assistance for political change in support of democratization proved quite contentious, with most participants agreeing that extreme caution be exercised in this area. One participant argued, "I stand to be convinced that there has been a conversion of principal donors, namely the United States. Yet there is a need for support to be obtained for certain areas, such as a dynamic civil society and the emergence of freedoms of association and expression. But will donor conditionalities be compatible with human rights? Conditions should not be ideologically loaded. How we do it should be up to us. In other words, we want donors to help us to be free. I'm glad there has been a change of approach, but I wonder if it is only transitory."

In support of the ideas that donors should not dictate the content of democracy, a number of participants thought that it might be helpful to indicate the "don'ts of donor involvement in democratization." One participant in the Addis workshop seemed to express the sentiments of the group there: "The external question is a touchy issue as regards the political side of democratization. External conditionality would be valid in the areas of facilitating the legal basis for free press and free speech and as regards the right of individuals to form groups or professional associations—the freedom of association. Donors should be concerned with these political areas and no others." Nevertheless, a number of concrete suggestions for related political areas, in which donors might be of help, were put forward, including the removal of dictators, the reduction of military assistance, and the promotion of civic groups.

Removal of Dictators

Participants suggested that donors might be able to help remove African dictators through open condemnation, quiet diplomacy, or sanctions. Clearly articulated statements by donors that openly denounce African dictators and antidemocratic forces, for example, could serve as manifestations of donors' unequivocal support for democracy. Participants pointed out that there has been an opening of the democratic process in countries targeted by such statements. Some participants also were of the opinion that external assistance could help ensure that democracy would not be subverted by disenchanted groups, such as defeated regimes or the military. They argued, however, that where aid donors have been ambiguous by sending contradictory signals, democratization has been delayed and, in some cases, leaders have refused outright to acquiesce to demands for political pluralism. It was offered that the threat of sanctions might be particularly useful for countries whose authoritarian regimes have a persistent record of human rights abuses. For such governments, sanctions would send a powerful message that undemocratic states that do not support democracy or respect human rights will be isolated and will risk having their economic lifelines severed.

Reduction of Military Assistance

A number of participants pointed out that African states have spent a significant percentage of their resources on military hardware and the military establishment, allegedly out of concerns for their national security and territorial integrity. Several argued that the disproportionate amount African budgets allocated to military spending had constrained the democratization process. Moreover, most participants were bitter that the legacy of the cold war competition was large military machines, be they supplied by Soviet or Western aid. One remarked: "We should be asking ourselves whether African countries, most of which are quite small, really have anything to secure. . . . One only needs a handful of paratroopers from Europe to take care of these armies and you start wondering whether the large military establishment in Africa is worth it."

Most participants advocated seeking the commitment of donors to limit or eliminate future military assistance to Africa and finance projects that could utilize military personnel in other sectors. Another suggestion was for donors to tie economic assistance to Africans undertaking to reduce military and defense spending. Nevertheless, participants were concerned that as the United States and the former Soviet Union start to downsize their militaries, they might increase efforts to export arms to developing countries, thereby supporting their own defense industries. Such action, participants argued, could thwart efforts to downsize African militaries and could therefore undermine the entire democratization process.

Promotion of Civic Groups

Participants in the three meetings believed that donors could assist the democratization process by pushing African governments to open a space or provide platforms of expression for civic groups, which would facilitate their active participation in society. One participant explained: "People talk about the silence of Africans and how they use their exit options rather than the voice option. What they do not understand is that it is difficult to use the voice option when there is no platform to raise one's voice. For example, because most of the news media are owned by the state, whatever voice or noise one makes cannot penetrate outside, which is a very serious issue." One suggestion was for donors to channel more aid to nongovernmental civic groups rather than governments: "Donors should identify the democratic forces in Africa and support them, because democracy can only be built around democrats. Assistance should not be channeled from government to government, but through nongovernmental organizations." A few participants disagreed completely: "In the past, the enormous effort and resources poured into assisting nongovernmental organizations has served to weaken them; they have become highly dependent, have not been able to increase their capacity, nor have they been able to relate successfully to other indigenous nongovernmental organizations. Also, it may well be that if you promote civic groups, you may also get greater fragmentation." In declaring that nongovernmental organizations are slow to react to authoritarian regimes and inefficient, one participant advocated that donors assist the private sector in Africa.

Improving Economic Conditions in Africa

There was identifiable agreement across the three workshops that donors would make a significant contribution to the democratization process by working to improve economic conditions in Africa. One participant, however, observed that external actors can become involved in a country's domestic politics by imposing conditionalities on countries in which economic institutions are not functioning because of a lack of good governance and internal democratic legitimacy. Such intervention, it was noted, has not been of much help to a majority of countries and, in some cases, has caused severe problems. Therefore, participants identified areas of assistance in which donor intervention might be extremely useful in improving economic conditions in Africa. These include forgiving African debt, reducing trade protectionism in the West, instituting fiscal reforms, focusing on human development, and countering capital flight.

Forgiving Debt

Participants preferred that donors forgive debt rather than grant new loans, arguing that donors do not assist in the development process by granting new loans when there are already large amounts of existing debt that needs to be serviced. They noted: "Donors are compounding the problem by giving new loans, especially to leaders who know their days in power are limited and live on their boats. . . . Instead of using these new loans to develop the country, they use it to further increase their personal wealth. . . ."

Reducing Western Trade Protectionism

Participants encouraged donors to reduce Western trade protectionism because many African countries have problems exporting their commodities. They argued that African economies will have little chance to improve or break their dependence on foreign aid if Western trade barriers deny them the opportunity to earn foreign exchange for commodities.

Instituting Fiscal Reforms

There was recognition that in order to ensure that African countries embark on genuine fiscal reforms, donors would have to impose conditionalities. Some participants suggested a further step would be to provide direct assistance toward the development of specialized skills in budget management. One observed: "In the colonial period, nationalists used to demand that there should be no taxation without representation, but today, I think the reverse point ought to be made: there should be no representation without taxation. . . The point I am making here is, in many African countries, 60 percent of the taxes that ought to be collected have not been collected. . . . You cannot sustain democracy on this type of situation."

A number of participants also argued that people often do not listen to government speeches pertaining to the budget because they are convinced that government always misappropriates money, most of which comes from foreign aid. Therefore, a number of participants advocated that, in the future, donor countries should explicitly tell African governments how they want their money spent: "If one is contributing about 30 percent of a budget, typically one should have some say in how that money is spent. Any debate on conditionality always should start with that premise." A few participants, however, cautioned that such aid is not charitable: "Assistance with those strings attached does not give one freedom. It's neocolonial and unfair for donors to determine where money is most needed."

Targeting Human Development

It was suggested that donors target most of their development assistance to improving basic needs—such as health, education, and food security, especially in countries plagued with severe drought and famine—in order to begin to facilitate the development of Africa's human resources. Given that at least 40 percent of African people live below the poverty level, participants thought it would be more appropriate to develop human capacities than to justify increased assistance for the purchase of military hardware. Although participants acknowledged that aid donors already assist in some of these areas, they thought it would be crucial for donors to begin to target more money for human development.

Capital Flight

Noting that capital flight is a severe drain on the economies of African countries, participants indicated that donor countries could mitigate the problem by reducing incentives given to some African leaders. Because donor countries have not always publicized their aid, they have unwittingly helped corrupt leaders and bureaucrats to transfer money out of their countries and into their personal accounts in the West. In the future, donors should make their aid transparent so people will know why and to whom assistance was given.

Assistance with Institutional Change

One of the problems identified in all workshops was the inability of African institutions to ensure accountability or to promote and protect the dignity and rights of the individual. Participants asked for help from donors in establishing the institutions necessary to sustain democracy such as constitutions and "critical" national institutions.

Constitutions

There was wide agreement that constitutional engineering would have to be undertaken in Africa. By borrowing from experiences of countries inside and outside Africa, defining and limiting government, developing rules that correspond to the problems recognized in Africa, a new covenant between state and society could be established. In this manner, it was hoped that many of the problems identified in the workshops might be addressed. For example, African leaders have in some cases manipulated constitutional provisions to consolidate power and get rid of their opponents. Participants were of the opinion that donors could play a key role in this process of helping to draft and review African constitutions, particularly in light of how they deal with issues of representation, ethnicity, presidential powers, elections, and individual and collective liberties. Scholars of jurisprudence, for example, could assist in examining why the limited government prescribed in colonial constitutions survived or did not. Still another role for donors could be to help facilitate within African countries widespread civic education regarding new constitutions. One participant noted that the "constitution means nothing if it cannot work. So civil society has an important role to play. In Madagascar, we won't let those in power play the same tricks tomorrow. We will call for accountability anytime a provision of the constitution is not applied. We have found that this is hard to do if individuals do not understand the constitution. That is why my association published a book on familiarization of issues of constitutionalism."

Critical National Institutions

Participants defined critical national institutions as the legislature, judiciary, the press, the electoral system and the civil service—institutions that have remained underdeveloped, and even undeveloped, in most African countries. The legislative and judicial branches of government, participants suggested, should be strengthened and made independent. They pointed out that, if individuals continue to associate these branches of government with the party or administration in power, then their trust in and the fairness of both branches will be severely jeopardized. Participants thought that donor assistance would be particularly useful in providing some of the means by which these branches could exercise their functions. For example, computers could help the judiciary and legislature build institutional memory. Donors also could help train the staff of these institutions and suggest elements that Africans could incorporate into new codes of conduct for the two bodies.

Participants also recognized that the effectiveness of the judicial and legislative branches required the presence of an independent press, a revamped electoral system, and a neutral civil service—institutions that have been underutilized or nonexistent in most African countries. Requesting donor assistance in order to realize the potentials of these institutions, one participant cautioned, "I think there is a very serious danger that we may have a swing and a back-swing in the democratization process if we do not have these institutions developed. There will be a swing, for example, when people say, 'We have had multipartyism with little in terms of outcomes.' Then, there will be a swing the other way when they say, 'We had it, it didn't work, so let us go back to what we had originally.'"

The Press

As an independent press was considered key to achieving open society, participants thought that donors could be particularly helpful in providing funding for the establishment of private African presses, especially where governments currently control all information distributed to the public. In countries with private print and broadcast media, it was offered that donors still could help update technology in order to improve the quality of print and increase the area of distribution.

Civil Service

Concerned that the civil service in Africa has been plagued with corruption and nepotism and has been politicized under authoritarian regimes, participants indicated that donors might be able to help overhaul the civil service, suggesting ways to make it neutral, effectively decentralized, and well paid. Noting that the ability of the civil service to make impartial decisions or to implement important policies is under serious question, participants suggested that donor assistance might help Africans improve the professionalism of civil servants in these areas. One remarked: "Current efforts at structural reforms in Africa will likely fail unless the capacity of the civil service to implement policy analysis and policy implementation is improved. . . . Until this happens, we are likely to just be wasting our time."

Electoral Systems

Participants noted that improving the electoral system in African countries in which elections have been associated with rigging, intimidation, and violence would constitute significant headway toward democratization and improved governance. Sending observers to African countries when elections are held in order to ensure that voting is free and fair helps elect the peoples' candidates to office, but it does not help sustain the system if foreign observation is necessary to guarantee legitimacy. Instead, it was suggested that donor countries should train Africans in observing and monitoring their own elections as well as in the procedures for efficient voter registration.

Greater Utilization of African Talent

Participants were of the opinion that donors should respect and utilize African talent, particularly because African experts often have more practical experience than Western experts sent to Africa by donors. Participants argued that, in the past, too many Western experts with only theoretical knowledge have been sent to African countries to make recommendations for improving conditions there, and their lack of practical experience in given countries has led them to make recommendations that have not really been helpful. Participants also associated the brain drain in African countries to the lack of in-country utilization of indigenous talent; highly skilled individuals in search of expert positions move to Western countries to accept jobs they cannot find in their own countries. Consequently, participants want donor countries to help them utilize and mobilize local African talent whenever possible to prevent the continuous brain drain.

Inter-African Exchange of Information on Democratization

Participants suggested that one of the major areas of donor assistance to Africans could be in facilitating the exchange of information among African countries, perhaps through regional or continental institutions. One participant commented: "One of the important values of these workshops has been that we are sharing information. But, this also demonstrates the lack of information sharing in Africa, as well as the lack of efforts to use what has happened within and outside the continent in the past and apply it to the current situation. I will give one example: Nigeria adopted the open-ballot system a few years after a number of countries moved away from it. Some of the problems Nigeria is now discovering perhaps could have been avoided if policy makers had known the reasons why other countries had moved away from the open-ballot system. . . . This is what I mean by the lack of information among African countries." In the Namibia workshop, participants asked for assistance in ensuring that the exchange of information among African participants, evident in the deliberations, would not end with the Namibian workshop. African participants held several informal meetings culminating in the formation of the Transnational African Democratic Center. One concrete proposal they offered was for donors to fund network-building activities in Africa such as the newly established Transnational African Democratic Center.

Inter-African Cooperation

Participants suggested that aid donors could assist African countries in solving problems of democratization by promoting inter-African cooperation, particularly as regards the sharing of resources. Participants noted that by acting jointly they might begin to solve problems, such as the downsizing of African militaries, economic decline, and fair elections. One remarked: "When the colonists were in Africa, they tried to get African countries to act together on a number of common areas, such as examinations, universities, elections, research, and a number of other institutions. Unfortunately, with independence, all these institutions were nationalized and then disintegrated. Today, however, it seems as if it is becoming clearer and clearer that given the resource base of the various African governments and the fact that we are all drawing from the same place, it may be necessary to take up this strategy again."

In conclusion, donor assistance in promoting and sustaining democracy in Africa is important, but, as one participant put it, "donors should exercise care not to dictate, impose, or predetermine the content of democracy. They should tie conditionality, if any, to policy performance, not to ideological orientation or to a specific blueprint for democracy." They must stop sending mixed signals and should agree to accept the autonomy of the democracies that emerge. This concern was aptly expressed by a participant in the Addis Ababa workshop who emphasized the need for clarity of conditions between donors and recipients. He noted that the relationship was one of a "marriage of convenience," in which Africans are seeking aid and donors demanding accountability. He emphasized that in such a relationship both sides needed to understand the terms of the relationship needed to promote democracy and economic development.

Conclusion: Role of Africans in the Democratization Process

The three workshops revealed common views on some of the important needs and problems faced by newly democratizing countries. There was some expectation that there will be regional variations on some issues but the overall consistency and commonality in views toward democracy was surprising to most of the participants. Participants acknowledged the crucial role Africans have to play in making the democracy movement continue, gain strength, or weaken. As has been noted throughout this report, external support in the right directions can help to ease the pain of transition to democracy, but the role played by Africans themselves is what is important in sustaining and consolidating it. One participant stated, "I think the ability of people to challenge the government to be responsive to popular will and face the reality of that challenge is what I think the issue is in a democracy. . . . From colonial times, somebody has always said, we will do the job for you, and I think the challenge of democracy is to say let the people face some challenges themselves. . . . They can be assisted at best, but nobody can do it for them."

The importance of Africans' inventing a credible alternative model to the Western model of democracy was underscored as crucially important: "One can take as a starting point a universal model and then add to it the very specific characteristics of the continent we are dealing with. . . . In other words, democracy can generate certain contradictions and that is why we have to be constantly aware of what might happen and try to manage the contradictions." Another participant focused his arguments specifically on the evolution of democracy in Africa: "When I talk about the evolution of democracy, I don't mean something that can come from one day to the next. . . . It is something that needs to continuously evolve and continuously change. . . . It is only through this constant evolution and development that we can achieve democracy. . . . Democracy also means constantly involving the largest number of people in the management of their own affairs. . . . In order to do this, we have to ensure that different organizations come into being and citizens become aware of what is happening, of what the different organizations represent and help them conquer power. . . . In other words, the different organizations have to form a sort of relay system or bridge to coordinate and support the process." In short, there was consensus in all three meetings that for democracy to survive in Africa there should be a commitment to the concept, the value, and the goal of democracy at the individual as well as the group level.

There was also a suggestion that, rather than looking to the West for success stories on democracy, it would also be helpful to examine democratic experiments in Africa from countries such as Botswana, the Gambia, Mauritius, Senegal, and Zimbabwe, and other Third World nations (such as India and in Latin America) to analyze and draw lessons of concrete democratic practices that work in those countries. In addition to national examples, participants suggested there were also cases of development projects, institutions, and associations that have succeeded in some countries that should be emulated. One participant took exception to this suggestion and argued, "The few country examples just mentioned proves that we find success stories only in the small states where there is no problem of communication, and in European countries, democracy prevailed only when these countries reached a certain economic level. . . . I am worried because it seems to me the fundamental requirement is economic because democracy is most of all a matter of decentralization and participation, but decentralization and participation require communication, means of communication so that everybody can talk to each other, know each other and there is a free flow of information on every side. . . . The reason why we in Africa have different problems is due to the fact that perhaps we want to set an order of priorities for installing democracy, but we want to stress the importance of developing infrastructures which will enable people to communicate freely and which will enable the press and media to spread democratic culture leading to greater success."

Although there was consensus in all workshops that Africans have to take the lead in the transition to democracy, it was also agreed that there is a need for external actors in helping to tackle the problems in Africa. When external actors take definitive steps, such as in Kenya, there are positive results toward democracy. Zaire has been slow in progressing towards democracy primarily because donors have not been definitive in their actions. Participants noted the need for coherence and collaborative efforts on the part of donors in helping African countries in democratization.

Although the issues threatening democracy in Africa and the disagreements among participants on how to tackle them have been discussed throughout this report, it is important in these concluding pages to highlight major differences in approaches, which stem from the fact that there is no single established method of tackling these issues. The methods used to address such problems as the role of the military, replacing dictators, the number of political parties, managing ethnicity, and the appropriate role of donors will vary from country to country, depending on the degree of significance placed on them by the individual countries.

Participants' views regarding the role of the military in the democratization process usually reflected the experiences within their country. Suggestions included keeping the military out of politics, downsizing the military, giving it civic responsibilities or redirecting its efforts into productive sectors of the economy, and professionalizing it. Some even questioned the necessity of maintaining militaries in Africa at all. Thus, although the disagreements were mainly centered around how to deal with the military as a major contestant for political power in Africa, there was the underlying assumption among participants of the need for effective civilian control of the military in Africa.

The discussions on how to replace dictators in Africa and whether Western countries should be involved brought about a lot of divergent opinions and suggestions. Two key suggestions that emerged from these discussions basically summarize the different approaches. First, there must be a provision in the constitution that limits the powers and tenure of leaders, and it should also indicate clearly how they can be replaced before their terms end constitutionally. This suggestion was advanced particularly because of the argument that, if a dictator is elected to office, then the laws of the country have to be respected and it is not legitimate to use unconstitutional means to replace him, such as coups d'état by military officers, which has been a common device used in African countries. The second suggestion disagreed with relying on constitutional provisions primarily because they have not worked in those African countries where dictators have total control of the armed forces and are willing to use them against those who question their authority. One participant argued, "What should we do if these guarantees in the constitution do not work and you cannot get rid of the dictators? . . . I will submit that the people are the last guarantee. . . . They are the sovereign and they have the right to assume their responsibilities by fighting for their rights." Another participant mentioned that "in some countries, the Supreme Court has the power to put an end to the rule of the President, but the structure of the forces in African countries is such that the members of the court are the ones who might get arrested if they attempt to do such a thing. . . . Therefore, what we need to do is to call outside help by turning to donors to help us get rid of the dictators by whatever means necessary." The suggestion of relying on donors for help to overthrow dictators was brushed aside by some participants who pointed out that donors have been particularly helpful in sustaining some dictators rather than helping to get rid of them and should not be trusted.

Another area of major disagreement by participants had to do with the role, number, and financing of political parties in African countries. Although in the Benin workshop a participant from Nigeria explained the rationale behind the adoption of the open-ballot system and the imposition of only two parties in his country, other participants were not convinced that it was the best method of minimizing electoral fraud and political fragmentation. With regard to running for public office and financing political parties, some participants pointed out that running for office in African countries, as in other countries, costs money and it seems that only those with money can afford to do this. One participant argued, "Only those that can get hold of finance can manage their campaigns and nobody focusses on how they get the money. . . . If democracy is only for those who have money, then where are we going? . . . We have to be able to find some solution and public funds have to be made use of in a loyal fashion." The discussions on number of parties and how to minimize electoral fraud did not reach consensus, and the onus was left on individual countries to tackle the problems based on what they thought was the most appropriate method.

The question of how to manage ethnicity was also a contentious issue in all three workshops. Some participants argued that promoting ethnicity was not an obstacle to democracy, while others felt strongly that the strength of ethnicity has to be recognized because continued suppression of ethnic identities could lead to severe problems. Federalism, it was noted, is a mechanism to manage ethnic conflict, but under federalism the disagreement was whether there should be more decentralization or devolution of power. Addressing the issue of ethnicity especially in a federal system and how to share power was probably the most contentious issue in all three workshops.

It is also important by way of conclusion to mention the paradox of democracy produced from outside. Essentially, democracy can only come from inside, and the amount that external actors can and should do to encourage it must inherently be limited. "Democratic" governments helped to power by external forces may be liable to lose support, because they are seen as being the stooges of foreign powers. One participant raised the question, "What responsibilities do the donors assume when they are encouraging (or even forcing) African states to adopt 'democracy'?" In response to this question, another participant argued, "Having helped to create democracy, external powers must then be prepared to respect it. . . . You cannot assume that the interests of African peoples, reflected in their democratic governments are the same as those of wealthy external powers. . . . Having helped to establish such governments, external powers have a minimal obligation not to destabilize them, and a broader obligation to help democratic governments achieve the popular aspirations, without which democracy will surely fail."

Appendix

Workshop Participants

WORKSHOP I: COTONOU, BENIN

GRACE D'ALMEIDA ADAMON is an attorney and an advocate of democracy in Benin. She served on the High Council for the Republic, which was the team that directed the transition.

AUGUSTINE AINAMOU is a professor at the Université Nationale de Bénin in Cotonou.

TESSY BAKARY is professor of political science at the University of Laval in Quebec, Canada.

S.B. DARAMY is currently labor adviser in the Ministry of Labor in Sierra Leone. He is a political scientist specializing in African politics.

OLATUNJI DARE is chair of the editorial board of *The Guardian* newspaper in Nigeria. *The Guardian* is one of Nigeria's most influential newspapers, with a circulation of 90,000. He is on leave from the University of Lagos, where he is a senior lecturer in journalism. He has written extensively on transition programs in Africa and the democratic process.

JONGWANE DIPOKO is president of the university staff union and a professor of physics at the University of Yaounde in Cameroon.

LEOPOLD DOSSOU is a history professor at the Université Nationale de Bénin in Cotonou and secretary of the country's trade unions.

ROBERT DOSSOU is a professor at the Université Nationale de Bénin in Cotonou. He is the former secretary of the Study and Research Group on Democracy and Economic and Social Development in Africa (GERDDES-

Africa), an organization that is playing an active role in promoting and monitoring the progress of democracy, especially within the West African subregion.

J. ISAWA ELAIGWU is professor of political science at the University of Jos in Nigeria. His research focuses on civil-military relations in Nigeria.

BAGNAN AISSATA FALL is minister for development and women's affairs for the Nigerian government and former head of women's affairs at the USTN (Federation of Nigerian Labor Unions). She was also president of the sociocultural committee of the Nigerian National Conference.

FELIX IROKO is assistant dean of the faculty of letters and history professor at the Université Nationale de Bénin in Cotonou.

LAMINE KAMARA is an advocate of democracy and civil society in Guinea.

JOSEPH KIZERBO is secretary for international relations of the National Convention of Progressive Patriots (CNPP) in Burkina Faso and an internationally renowned historian and scholar.

AMBROISE KOM is a civil rights activist and professor of African literature at the University of Yaounde in Cameroon. He heads a private organization of teachers and professionals that concentrates on human rights issues.

RENE LEMARCHAND is professor at the University of Florida and first director of the university's African Studies Center.

JACQUESSON MAZETTE is secretary general of the teachers union that has been central to the democratization effort in Central African Republic.

MARIE GENEVIEVE NDOUTOUME is counselor to the Minister of Territorial Administration in Gabon, which handles the organization of elections, the registration of parties, and related tasks.

NZONGOLA NTALAJA is professor of African studies at Howard University in Washington, D.C.

HUMPHREY NWOSU is chair of the National Electoral Commission in Nigeria.

DELE OLOWU is professor of political science in the Department of Public Administration at Obafemi Awolowo University in Nigeria.

ALAO A. SADIKOU is president of the Study and Research Group on Democracy and Economic and Social Development in Africa (GERDDES-Africa), headquartered in Benin.

RAYMOND SOCK is the former solicitor general of the Gambia and currently director of the African Center for Democracy and Human Rights Studies (ACDHRS).

ELISEE SOUMONNI is chair of the history department at the Université Nationale de Bénin in Cotonou. His work has focused on political pluralism in Africa.

STEVE SWARAY is currently acting governor of the Bank of Sierra Leone. He is an economist who formerly worked for the Mano River Union in

Sierra Leone. He was a member of the constitutional review committee that recommended reintroduction of a multiparty system in Sierra Leone.

ALBERT TEVOEDJRE is a professor at the Université Nationale de Bénin and a former senior official of an international labor organization.

NICOLAS VAN DE WALLE is an assistant professor in the Department of Political Science and African Studies at Michigan State University.

HERBERT F. WEISS is professor of political science at the City University of New York and coordinator of the Central Africa Project at the Institute of African Studies at Columbia University.

PAULETTE YAMBO-DUSSAUD is a journalist and advocate of democracy and political pluralism in the Congo.

WORKSHOP II: ADDIS ABABA, ETHIOPIA

NETSANET ASFAW is a member of Relief and Rehabilitation Commission (RRC) and the Central Committee of the Ethiopia People's Revolutionary Democratic Front (EPRDF).

CHRISTOPHER CLAPHAM is professor and chair of the Department of Politics and International Relations, Lancaster University, England, and vice-president of the African Studies Association of the United Kingdom.

AMEDEE DARGA is a member of the Mauritius Legislative Assembly and active in municipal politics, having served recently as mayor of Curepipe, one of the largest cities in Mauritius.

TERESA SMITH DE CHERIF is manager and senior editor of the Africa Bureau Information Center of the U.S. Agency for International Development.

FATOUMATA SIRE DIAKITE is president and founder of the Association for the Advancement and Protection of Malian Women's Rights.

F.K. DRAH is senior lecturer in political theory and African politics in the political science department at the University of Ghana in Legon.

FILOMENA DOS SANTOS is adviser to the Secretary of State for Internal Administration in Cape Verde.

BECHIR El-HASSAN is chair of the Human Rights Committee of the Union des Forces Démocratiques in Mauritania.

J. ISAWA ELAIGWU is professor of political science at the University of Jos in Nigeria. His research focuses on civil-military relations in Nigeria.

ALMAZ ESHETE is director of the Center for Research and Training for Women in Development and chair of the Psychology Department at Addis Ababa University.

DAVID FASHOLE-LUKE is currently associated with the Economic Commission for Africa in Addis Ababa, Ethiopia. He is also a professor of political science at Dalhousie University in Canada.

GRACE GITHU is president of the Kenyan Branch of the Federation of Women Lawyers (FIDA).

MELVENIA GUEYE is a staff member of the Africa Subcommittee, Committee on Foreign Affairs, U.S. House of Representatives, U.S. Congress.

F.A. HARRIS is director of the Office of Regional African Affairs of the U.S. Department of State.

GITOBU IMANYARA is editor of the *Nairobi Law Monthly* and a human rights activist. He was the 1991 recipient of the Louis M. Lyon Award for conscience and integrity in journalism, given by the Nieman Foundation at Harvard University.

RUTH IYOB is postdoctoral fellow at the Institute of African Studies at Emory University in Atlanta.

LENCHO LETA is deputy secretary general of the Oromo Liberation Front (OLF) and represents his organization on the council that is in charge of Ethiopia's transitional government.

ABDUL MOHAMMED is director of the Inter-Africa Group, a center for dialogue on humanitarian, peace, and development issues in the Horn of Africa, with its headquarters in Addis Ababa, Ethiopia.

NAMULI MUWANGA is deputy executive secretary of the Uganda Human Rights Activists.

BEN ODOKI is a member of the Uganda Constitutional Commission.

ARTHUR ODER is a member of the Supreme Court in Uganda.

KASSIM SAID is a medical doctor who was one of the founding members of Tribune Libre, a club that provided a meeting place throughout the 1980s for democracy-minded intellectuals, and founder of the Mouvement pour la Renovation et l'Action Democratic Party (MOURAD), which promotes multiparty democracy in Comoros.

HAILU SHOWEL is a prominent lawyer in Ethiopia.

KAPEPWA ITALIKA TAMBILA is professor of history on the Faculty of Arts and Social Sciences at the University of Dar Es Salaam in Tanzania.

ERNEST WAMBA-DIA WAMBA is associate professor of history in the Faculty of Arts and Social Sciences at the University of Dar Es Salaam in Tanzania.

JENNIFER WINDSOR is with the Africa Bureau of the U.S. Agency for International Development.

KIFLE WODAJO is a member of Parliament in Ethiopia.

TESHOME WOLDE-MARIAM is a prominent human rights lawyer in Ethiopia.

TAYE WOLDE-SEMIAT is professor in the Department of Political Science and International Relations at Addis Ababa University.

ARISTIDE ZOLBERG is professor at the Graduate Faculty of Social and Political Science of the New School for Social Research in New York City.

WORKSHOP III: WINDHOEK, NAMIBIA

OTILLIE ABRAHAMS is a member of the Namibian National Front (NNF) and also involved in grass roots issues, particularly human rights, education, and national reconciliation.

HUGH AFRICA is an academic who was formerly involved with training programs of the United Nations Institute in Namibia. He is also active in the Namibian Economic Planning Research Unit (NEPRU).

JOEL BARKAN is with the Regional Economic Development Services Office for East and Southern Africa (REDSO/ESA) of the U.S. Agency for International Development in Nairobi.

ERIC BIWA is one of four parliamentary members of the United Democratic Front of Namibia (UDF).

NARISON BODA is a member of Groupement Libérale de Madagascar, a human rights organization in Madagascar.

CHAKUFWA CHIHANA is secretary general of the Southern Africa Trade Unions Coordinating Council (SATUCC) and is from Malawi. He is the recipient of the 1992 Robert F. Kennedy Human Rights Award.

CHRISTOPHER CLAPHAM is professor and chair of the Department of Politics and International Relations, Lancaster University, England, and vice-president of the African Studies Association of the United Kingdom.

TERESA SMITH DE CHERIF is manager and senior editor of the Africa Bureau Information Center of the U.S. Agency for International Development.

DAWOOD DITHATO is a staff member of the Democracy Research Project at the University of Botswana.

MARGARET DONGO is a member of Parliament and of the ruling Zimbabwean African National Union—Patriotic Front (ZANU-PF) in Zimbabwe.

ANDRE DU TOIT is a professor of political studies at the University of Cape Town, South Africa.

FRED C. FISCHER is director of the Regional Economic Development Services Office for East and Southern Africa (REDSO/ESA) of the U.S. Agency for International Development in Nairobi.

ANNA FRANK is parliamentary member of the official opposition party, the Democratic Turnhalle Alliance of Namibia (DTA) and one of only four women in the National Assembly.

BENES GWANAS is Namibia's first female attorney. She is a member of the Public Service Commission and is interested in human rights issues.

F.A. HARRIS is director of the Office of Regional African Affairs of the U.S. Department of State.

LAURAH HARRISON is chair of the National Women's Lobby Group in Zambia, which participated in monitoring the recent elections.

PETER KATJAVIVI is vice-chancellor designate of the University of Namibia. He was involved in the negotiations leading to independence as an activist in South West African People's Organization (SWAPO) and later a delegate to the Constituent Assembly.

EDMOND KELLER is professor of political science at the University of California at Los Angeles.

IAN LIEBENBERG is senior researcher at the Group Social Dynamics Unit: Constitutional and Political Affairs, of the Human Sciences Research Council in South Africa.

DAMBUZA LUKHELE is a Swaziland senator as well as a chief and a businessman.

JABULANE MATSEBULA is editor of *The Times* of Swaziland, the country's sole privately owned daily newspaper.

HILARIO MATUSSE is secretary general of the National Organization of Journalists and chief editor of Televisao Experimental (TVE) in Mozambique.

MODICAI MSISHA is secretary general of the Malawi Law Society.

FESTUS NAHOLO is deputy chief coordinator for the South West African People's Organization (SWAPO) in Namibia.

DELE OLOWU is professor of political science in the Department of Public Administration at Obafemi Awolowo University in Nigeria.

ELYETT RASENDRATSIROFO is director of international affairs at the Observatoire Nationale de la Démocratie in Madagascar.

DONALD ROTHCHILD is professor of political science at the University of California at Davis.

FOSTON SAKALA is chair of the Zambian Election Monitoring Coordinating Committee (ZEMCC), which monitored the recent elections.

CALEB SELLO heads the Lesotho Council of nongovernmental organizations and is a former Foreign Ministry official.

MASIPULA SITHOLE is associate professor and former chair of the Department of Political and Administrative Studies at the University of Zimbabwe.

ZOLA SKWEYIYA is director of the Legal and Constitutional Affairs Department of the African National Congress in South Africa.

PETER SMITH is associated with the Inkatha Institute in South Africa.

FATOU SOW is a sociologist at the Institut Fondamental de l'Afrique Noire (IFAN), a major research center at the Cheikh Anta Diop University in Dakar.

G. TOTEMEYER is head of the Department of Public Administration and Political Studies at the University of Namibia.

FREIDA WILLIAMS is secretary of the Ministry of Youth and Sports in Namibia.

NOEL YAO is chef de service international at *Fraternité-Matin*, the principal daily newspaper in Côte d'Ivoire.

NATIONAL RESEARCH COUNCIL STAFF

DIANE GOLDMAN is administrative associate for the Division of Social and Economic Studies.

SAHR JOHN KPUNDEH is senior research associate for the Panel on Issues in Democratization.

LOIS PETERSON is research assistant for the Panel on Issues in Democratization.

SUSANNE STOIBER is director of the Division of Social and Economic Studies.

MARY E. THOMAS is senior program assistant for the Panel on Issues in Democratization.

(The staff attended all three workshops.)